A Priestless People?

D1344784

A Priestless People?

A *new vision for the Catholic priesthood*

Vincent McLaughlin

CANTERBURY
PRESS
Norwich

© Vincent and Imelda McLaughlin 1998

First published in 1998 by The Canterbury Press Norwich
(a publishing imprint of Hymns Ancient & Modern Limited
a registered charity)
St Mary's Works, St Mary's Plain
Norwich, Norfolk, NR3 3BH

All rights reserved. No part of this publication which is
copyright may be reproduced, stored in a retrieval system,
or transmitted, in any form or by any means, electronic,
mechanical, photocopying, recording, or otherwise, without
the prior permission of the publisher.

British Library Cataloguing in Publication Data

A catalogue record for this book is available
from the British Library

ISBN 1-85311-193-7

Typeset by Rowland Phototypesetting and
printed in Great Britain by Biddles Ltd
Guildford and King's Lynn

Contents

Acknowledgements

I would like to thank Christine Smith and Vicky Acklam for their careful editing and constant help with this book.

Also, those friends from the parishes in which Vincent served who so encouraged him in his writing, and all my family and friends who have supported me in this work, and finally I would like to thank Dr Michael Winter for giving of his time to write the foreword.

Foreword

The 1980's was a period of intellectual triumph for the Catholic Church. During that decade, half a dozen Catholic priests occupied professorial chairs of theology and allied subjects in various British universities, together with the mastership of one of Oxford's most famous colleges. This galaxy of talent was merely the tip of the iceberg. Other priests were lecturing in less prominent university positions. The anomaly is that all of them had resigned from the active ranks of the priesthood and most of them had married.

This haemorrhage of talent raises serious questions for the Catholic community. Clearly the emotional lives of these scholars had been frustrated while they lived within the ranks of the clergy but what of their intellectual abilities? One is left with the uneasy feeling that the Church's regime may have constrained their brains as well as their hearts.

It is within this context that Vincent McLaughlin's book needs to be appreciated. He too was a scholar whose considerable abilities flourished after he had resigned from the priesthood and married. It is a pleasure for me to commend this book to the public. I knew him both at school and in the seminary. That latter place at which our paths crossed is significant. Both of us had chosen to proceed to the priesthood; neither of us had chosen to study at that particular seminary. We had been sent there by the bishop without any choice on our part. From then on every significant decision about our studies and pastoral work was made by the authorities without our consent or even consultation.

Does it have to be thus? A glance at the Anglican system reveals a different practice which is more humane and more satisfactory for the individuals and for the Church as a whole. If accepted, ordination candidates can apply to a theological college or course which they have decided upon themselves. Once ordained, the first curacy is normally in the diocese which sponsored them, but thenceforward they are entitled to seek work in any Anglican diocese. No constraints are placed upon the type of work which they might choose within the ecclesiastical system, be it parish work, education or social work, such as a prison chaplaincy for example. Should they wish to pursue further studies it is not only permitted, but facilitated.

The result is that they have a generally contented clergy who are enabled to develop all aspects of their personalities, thus enriching their service of God. One sees many distinguished scholars in the ranks of the Anglican clergy and, more to the point, several first-class theologians in their episcopate.

Among the Catholic clergy there are many frustrated lives. Those who know the system well are aware of how many talented priests there are who never achieve their full potential because their superiors will not allow them the opportunities to develop. It is in this context of repressive legalism that the law of compulsory celibacy must be evaluated. Contrary to superficial perceptions, it is not the only constraint placed upon the lives of the priests: possibly it is the worst because it is the denial of a basic human right.

Although the issue of celibacy has been debated openly for more than twenty years, Vincent McLaughlin's book is a welcome addition to the discussion, which in this country has been conducted mostly in articles in specialist journals, newspapers, and the autobiographies of those who have resigned. A full scale treatment of the question, such as is presented in these pages, has long been overdue.

As long as open debate continues there is hope for the future. The present situation contains nought for our comfort. The law of celibacy is still imposed on candidates seeking ordination from within the Catholic community. It has received no serious theological justification, and nearly all dioceses are ordaining married converts from the Anglican clergy. One is reminded of the Marxist allegation about capitalism, namely that its intrinsic contradictions must eventually bring about its collapse.

Apart from their implied statements of intent, latent in their ordaining married converts, the bishops' attitude is characterized by total silence. It is disturbing. Possibly it represents what the psychiatrists call denial. That is to say, when the problem is too overwhelmingly difficult to cope with the individual pretends to himself (subconsciously) that it does not exist, and will neither speak about it, nor face up to it in any way.

Another possibility is that the Pope has forbidden them to discuss the question, which leaves one wondering which is worse: the Pope's high handed attitude or their acquiescence to the curtailment of responsibilities which belong rightfully to their office as successors of the apostles.

Totally inadequate numbers of candidates are coming forward for the secular priesthood. Increasing numbers of parishes lack adequate staffing. The logical outcome is clear, but the only way out of the morass of self-inflicted wounds is enlightened debate, to which the present volume is a welcome contribution.

Michael M. Winter
September, 1997

Preface

It is difficult to resist the impression that many ordinary Catholics, especially though not only those in middle or later years, are somewhat bewildered by aspects of our Church. From Pope John Paul II and some other leading figures in the Church they hear, and often welcome, the familiar voice of authority bringing the certainty and security which were once the most characteristic and comforting features of the Roman Catholic Church. But we are also vividly aware of other voices sounding a very different tune. No longer do papal and episcopal utterances go unchallenged. Neither is this critical stance restricted to a tiny group of dissident theologians: unrest is widespread. The Catholic person in the pew is dismayed by reports not only of sexual abuse by priests and religious but also of ecclesiastical authority's attempts to cover it up. Church congregations, brought up for generations to believe that clerical celibacy is the irreplaceable bastion and inner strength of priestly devotion, are now instructed that it can be set aside to facilitate the admission to membership and Holy Orders of former Church of England clergymen prompted to come over to Rome by the English section of the Church of England's decision to ordain women. Dissent from official moral teaching, especially over contraception, is now openly proclaimed, dissent – according to a report in *The Tablet* (15 July 1995) – remarkably endorsed by the German edition of the new Catechism. 500,000 Catholics from Austria, hitherto regarded as a centre of conservative orthodox opinion, have signed a protest against certain official teachings and policies. Even *The Universe* newspaper carries articles and letters critical of the official Church. At the same time, priests are resigning, retiring or dying and are not being replaced. What, some Catholics are asking, has become of Christ's promise to Peter that the gates of hell would not prevail against his Church?

Many of us grieve deeply to see the ability of our Church to preach the Gospel to our spiritually needy world being undermined by these tensions and dissensions. I have not, however, written this book as a rallying call to return to a past which is gone. It is a simple plea to all who love the Church to think and to pray hard about our present problems. I hope that no one who takes the trouble to read this book will be dismayed to find in it criticisms of aspects of Church life, teaching and management policies. Thirty years ago, the Second Vatican Council's document 'The Church' observed that 'An individual layman, by reason of the knowledge, competence or outstanding ability which he may enjoy, is permitted and sometimes even obliged to express his opinion on things which concern the good of the Church' (Abbott, ed., *The Documents of Vatican II*, p. 64). Ironically, it is the failure of the Church authorities to implement the provisions of the very next sentence, 'when occasions arise, let this be done through the agencies set up by the Church for this purpose', which is the source of so much frustration and anger: there simply are no such agencies. That Church authority has not yet rid itself of the fear of constructive criticism is amply demonstrated by *The Tablet*'s report (15 July 1995) of Cardinal Danneels' impassioned plea for a fully educated and informed laity: asked by a reporter what would be his attitude towards those educated and well-informed laity who arrived at conclusions which differed from those of Church authority, the Cardinal replied, 'If you come to a different conclusion, study more.' We cannot hope that the laity will be taken seriously until the authorities in the Church themselves take seriously Cardinal Hume's conviction: 'If I say things must change, it means I must change' (*The Tablet*, 22 July 1995).

This book carries my name as author and the first person personal pronoun used throughout is usually 'I'. This is due to the desire to simplify presentation and expression. The book is as much my wife's as my own, not simply in the sense that she has shared in the writing, has read and re-read every word of the drafts and constructively criticized throughout, but much more deeply in that it is the fruit of our shared experience. We are both cradle Catholics who grew up separately in the Church but who, since we have known and loved each other, have discovered a common love for our Church which yearns to see its treasures made available to the world openly, freely and without fear. We hope that we have made a start in offering to our fellow Catholics these thoughts on the priesthood. It is our earnest and sincere hope that they will, in however small a way, help to free our Church from the bonds of prejudice and fear which we believe are strangling its Gospel mission.

Vincent McLaughlin
July 1995

I

A Chronic Shortage of Priests

The Priests were too few . . .
(2 Chronicles 29:34)

There must be few Roman Catholics who are unaware that all is not well with our Church. This was brought home vividly on the Sunday before the publication of Pope John Paul II's Encyclical *Veritatis Splendor* in 1994, when the Bishops of England and Wales published a preliminary pastoral letter. It was sufficiently novel in 1968 to have had bishops issuing a defence of a papal encyclical after it had been published; now, we had bishops publishing a defence *before* publication. Nevertheless, in the welter of such controversies, I am not sure that too many Catholics are aware of a far more threatening problem: namely, the accelerating shortage of priests to staff our parishes.

This is a phenomenon new to these islands. Most British Catholics are familiar with the shortage of priests in missionary territory. Visiting preachers, who appeal for vocations, prayers and funds, regularly regale congregations with stories of the heroic efforts of a handful of priests travelling thousands of miles across their vast parishes to provide their people with Mass at least once a year, consecrating large numbers of hosts so that the laity can at least receive Holy Communion at intervals until the next priestly visit. Now the crisis is on our own doorsteps and in our own church sanctuaries.

We have the growing experience of more and more parishes being compelled to close down their subsidiary churches – those chapels in outlying areas which meet the needs of small or isolated communities unable to reach their parish church: there are simply no longer the priests available to service them. And even where churches are not closed, complaints are rising about the ever increasing necessity to drop one or more of the Sunday Masses and to reschedule the rest because parishes which used to have three or more resident priests now have only one, and that one priest is perhaps responsible for several parishes. We shall see more and more cases like the parish of St Edmund in Millwall, east London, for example. There, the parish priest was given a new appointment in Hertfordshire, which is several miles to the north-west, across dense urban sprawl. Nevertheless, with others, he had for some time to continue to visit Millwall to celebrate Mass and to deal with administration. This bizarre arrangement was due, said a Westminster diocese Vicar General, to the shortage of priests (*The Tablet*, 25 September 1993).

This is a particular instance of an alarmingly widespread predicament. Delegates to the 1992 National Conference of Priests learned that in ten years' time, one-third fewer priests would be working in England and Wales, and in 20 years, two-thirds fewer.* A casual glance through the *National Catholic Directory* for 1997 reveals that even at present there is a high percentage of parishes served by

* The statistics just issued for 1997 continue to confirm this trend.

only one priest: in Southwark, for example, nearly 60 per cent. If the statistics are accurate, and there is no reason to doubt them, within less than ten years, nearly 20 per cent of Southwark's parishes could have no priest at all and in a further ten years, that number could have doubled. Southwark is not exceptional. The diocese of Nottingham has drafted a plan to provide for parishes which will be without priests in a few years' time. Of all its parishes in the diocese, approximately two-thirds would be cared for by either a resident priest or a team of priests; a tenth would have semi-retired or 'part-time' priests (that is, having commitments elsewhere) and the rest served by a priest from another parish, with nuns, permanent deacons or religious brothers supplying on-the-spot pastoral care. It is not envisaged that such care could include Mass or hearing confessions (*The Tablet*, 19 June 1993). Similar problems face the diocese of Aberdeen. Bishop Mario Conti has already stated that Sunday Mass is now no longer available in some parishes because of the shortage of priests and he is convinced that this will not be long in spreading to other parts of Scotland. The Aberdeen diocese has 26 regular priests, most of whom are over 60 years of age, serving 41 parishes. They are assisted by visiting priests.

I attempted to obtain statistics for priest populations in the dioceses of England and Wales, but most of the diocesan curias proved reluctant to furnish them. The seven which provided complete figures showed a 5 per cent reduction from 1990 to 1993. The more significant statistic is that these same dioceses recorded among them a total of six seminary students in their final year.

However, the full scale of the problem can be better gauged from the sobering realities of the situation in the archdiocese of Southwark. Between 1992 and 1997 only 19 priests were ordained for the archdiocese, and 34 have died over the same period. The number of priests who have left the ministry was seven. The current figures for seminary students offer little hope for an improvement in either the short or long term. Of the priests currently belonging to the diocese, the highest proportion was ordained over 30 years ago. Within 15 to 20 years, therefore, there will be a substantial reduction in the clerical workforce through retirement or death, a reduction which will not be made up by new ordinations.

There is no sign that future prospects are any better. One of the ways in which some dioceses are trying to plug the gaps is through the employment of priests from Eastern Europe and from third world countries. This is not a solution. Language and cultural differences may not be an obstacle to the provision of a valid Mass, but they are already creating considerable difficulty at the pastoral level. A Christian community whose vigour is derived from having the Eucharist at its centre will not be formed by the importation of a cultic figure empowered to perform a sacramental rite *for* the group. The present policy tends to enhance the perception of the priest as a semi-mystic being endowed with sacred powers which he can exercise altogether apart from the eucharistic community. The Eucharist is the *entire* community gathered around the Lord's table to celebrate his life, death and resurrection and is the heart and source of all its Christian activity. That will not be achieved by measures which risk conferring upon the priest a quasi-magical status entirely alien to an authentically Christian sacramental life.

The admission of 'convert' Anglican clergy to the

4

priesthood is also unlikely to provide a long-term remedy. In the nature of the case, this is a very limited resource. There is also grave hesitation in the Church leadership to admit married clergy to full parish responsibility. A pastoral letter to English Catholics, read on 2 July 1995, granted that 'in the near future, a number of married priests will be serving in different capacities within the life and mission of our Church. This may include parochial duties, but without the full responsibility that goes with the office of parish priest'. Once again, there may be cultural problems in attempting to integrate former Anglicans into the culture of the post-Vatican II Catholic Church. Aside from such matters as having to deny the validity of priestly orders in the Church of England and Rome's view that the best priesthood is a celibate priesthood, many Anglicans will bring with them a tradition of liturgical worship which, since Vatican II, has been largely discarded in the Roman Catholic Church; they may be dismayed by the dauntingly austere aspect of our current liturgical format and furnishings. Those who have enjoyed the spirit of freedom and tolerance which is characteristic of the Church of England may well find Rome's attempt to control in detail every aspect of the individual Roman Catholic's life, particularly their married life, a challenge to their enthusiasm for our Church. Those who see in Rome an unshakeable bastion of unchangeable doctrine and discipline may be equally dismayed to discover – as they will if they are truthfully instructed in the history of Roman Catholic teaching – just how much change has taken place and can take place in apparently fixed positions, and that exactly the same tensions exist within our Church at all levels – clerical and lay, episcopal and priestly – on as great a variety of doctrinal and moral issues as within their own Church. It will not have escaped the notice of more observant Anglicans that Cardinal Hume has offered no guarantee that women would *never* be ordained in our Church. Development of doctrine is a very versatile tool; papal 'last words' on any subject are notoriously subject to change.

Finally, it is only realistic to observe that an influx, large or small, of married priests into the ranks of our compulsorily celibate and not entirely contented clergy will do little to quell the growing restiveness of many Catholics, both clerical and lay, over this highly sensitive issue. As a cure for our vocations shortage, this particular remedy bids fair to raise more problems than it solves.

These shortages have come about for two reasons. The first is that over the last 30 years huge numbers of priests have resigned from the active ministry. According to David Rice's *Shattered Vows* (Blackstaff Press, 1991 – a detailed study of resignations from the priesthood), since the Second Vatican Council ended in 1965, 100,000 men have left the priesthood. That figure is almost a quarter of all the active priests in the world. David Rice says that the exodus continues, quoting the American sociologist Richard Schoenherr's reckoning that at present 42 per cent of all American priests do not celebrate the silver jubilee of their ordination. In other words, half of all American priests under the age of 60 have left. A similar picture emerges from studies in European countries and, although figures in Britain are hard to come by, it is not likely that our situation is any healthier. It is clear that it is not only the permanency of marriage which is in crisis: so is the permanency of ordination.

The second reason for the shortage is the drastic decline

in the West in the number of men studying for the priest-hood. Given the further certain decrease through retire-ment and death and the increase in world population, it is clear that the proportion of priests to people can only decline. In 1993, for instance, the last year for which official figures are available, according to the Vatican direc-tory *Annuario Pontificio*, the number of ordinations dropped sharply. The number of priests who died or left the priesthood was greater than the number of new ordina-tions, leaving the proportion of priests to Catholics, let alone world population figures, in a state of major decline. These figures obviously do nothing to alleviate the ever sharpening crisis in Western Europe, regarded in the past as an almost limitless source of priestly vocations. An article in *The Tablet* during the same year reported the dramatic reduction in the number of candidates for the priesthood in Germany and quoted a theology professor from Tübingen university predicting that future priests and lay theologians must expect to have up to seven parishes each to look after. There is little reason to suppose that our circumstances will be any better.

This is not without its importance for our relations with our fellow Christians in other Churches. In several non-Catholic Churches we are seeing a deepening awareness of the importance of the sacramental system in general and of the celebration of the Eucharist in particular. It will be tragic if just at the time when there is greater convergence among Christians on the Eucharist as the heart of our worship, the Catholic Church should find itself unable to respond fully to this prompting of the Holy Spirit because of the shortage of the necessary manpower.

We cannot selfishly rest in the comfortable thought that

the crisis lies in a relatively distant future: these sombre statistics suggest that it is likely to come upon us suddenly. The high average age of currently active priests must mean that large numbers can be expected to retire at more or less the same time; there are simply not the candidates with the qualifications which Canon Law requires to replace them in either the short or long term. This fact will change the character of the Church to which we have been long accustomed: the easy availability of priests in their presbyteries, as visitors in our homes or as ministers to the sick in hospital. Arrangements for baptisms, weddings and funerals will become much more difficult. It is true that deacons, special ministers of the Eucharist and lay pastoral assistants can do much to soften the impact, but there are two crucial areas where current official policies leave such substitutes powerless: sacramental absolution and the celebration of Mass. Perhaps the first is of less general consequence in these days of massive decline in the practice of the Sacrament of Reconciliation but, while there is depressing evidence of a serious decrease in the numbers attending Mass, there is no reason to suppose that practising Catholics will be indifferent to the deprivation of the weekly Sunday Mass, which still remains at the heart of authentic Catholic devotion. Perhaps it may be possible for those with cars and enough money to pay the ecological price to cope with a round trip of 30 to 40 miles in some areas to get to Mass every Sunday. But for the poor, the unemployed, the sick, the disabled and young large families, such a solution is hardly possible. In the end we shall see the heart begin to go out of our faith.

This book does not pretend to provide the solution to the problem. But I hope that it will contribute a useful response to this grave situation. There is no possibility of dealing with the crisis unless the Catholic community as a whole comes to some understanding of the answers to certain questions. First, why have so many priests resigned from the active ministry in the last 30 years? Second, why is there so dramatic a decline in the numbers of candidates for the priesthood, particularly in the West? Third, how effective are new selection procedures and training systems in seminaries today? Fourth, perhaps surprisingly and certainly most importantly, how real is the alleged shortage of vocations?

The reflections which follow offer to my fellow Catholics, especially my fellow 'ordinary' Catholics who perhaps are only now beginning to be aware that the Church they have known and loved for so long is facing a very uncertain future, some ideas which I hope they will think about, discuss widely and make a subject of their prayers. For what is at stake is nothing less than the mission of the Church, of the whole People of God, to bring home to our world torn by hate, destitution and despair, the healing and saving message of Jesus, the Son of God and mender of broken human hearts.

'Come to me all you who labour and are burdened and I will give you rest, for my yoke is easy and my burden light' are words which Matthew places on Jesus' lips (Matthew 11:28, 30). Our Church, which is part of the Church of Jesus Christ, labours in these days under the burden of deprivation of the Eucharist and of a priestly ministry apparently stretched far beyond its available resources. We need to consider prayerfully, humbly and courageously what is Jesus' will for his Church in these circumstances; to bring to our consideration all our intellect and will; and above all, our love for one another in the community of God's people together with our readiness to follow to the end the will of God, our Father and Mother in heaven, whose sole concern is our joy in the Divine Persons and in one another.

2

Celibacy: the Only Reason for Leaving the Priesthood?

We shall praise your love more than wine;
how right it is to praise you.

(Song of Songs 1:4b)

Most people, I imagine, presume that priests leave the ministry largely because they are unable or unwilling to observe the law of celibacy. Some critics go further and say that such inability or unwillingness is a sign that they never had a true vocation in the first place. In a BBC *Panorama* programme in May 1993, Cardinal José Sanchez, Prefect of Rome's Congregation for the Clergy, accepted the interviewer's statistics of priestly breaches of the celibacy rule but blandly asserted that these men could not have been genuinely called to the priesthood. If this were true, then the Church's procedures for the discernment of vocations and the training of candidates for the priesthood stand condemned by the very authority itself responsible for them.

Difficulties with the law of celibacy are undoubtedly a very powerful factor in priestly departures. But to make them the sole cause is grossly to oversimplify a hugely complex situation. Many Roman Catholics and, especially, the hierarchy, perceive the present crisis in the priesthood in terms not so much of celibacy as of fidelity: good and faithful priests abide by the law; the wicked and faithless leave to marry. As one of the 100,000 priests who, since 1965, have left the priesthood and married, I would say that my own experience suggests something far less naive than the catch-all explanation of sex as the source of priestly defection. It is probably true that if all priests were to observe strictly to the letter the detailed advice and rules they are given in the seminary about contact with women, the number of clerical departures would be drastically cut. Unfortunately, the exact observance of this advice and of these rules engenders not only an attitude to women which, in practice, shows them little courtesy and less compassion, treating them primarily as a danger to both chastity and charity, but also a priesthood which lacks maturity, spontaneity, warmth, freedom and a sense of reality. It is surely significant that these are precisely the criticisms so frequently levelled today against both many of the priests who remain and of those recently ordained.

It is frequently argued that priests are, and always have been, made fully aware of all the obligations entailed by ordination and that they have at least six years in the seminary to weigh up the decision. This argument ignores the religious and psychological realities of the system. I, for instance, had wanted to be a priest from a very early age. I knew that priests did not marry and so simply took it for granted that I would not do so either. Throughout my childhood, early youth, first years at work and national military service, I retained the vision of eventual ordination and therefore kept girls at arm's length for fear of risking my 'vocation'. Risk was the operative word. Girls were not persons in their own right but potential spiritual threats. All the customary paraphernalia of Catholic sexual morality, with its assertions of instant mortal sin where there is the slightest wilful consent to the least sexual arousal – teaching certainly not abandoned by the new *Catechism of the Catholic Church* – bore upon me with redoubled force, insisting that if girls could so easily lead any Catholic male into mortal sin, how absolutely necessary it was that a Catholic male who was resolved upon the priesthood should take every step necessary to preserve his baptismal purity.

When, therefore, I accepted ordination, I fondly imagined that I was freely accepting celibacy too. In fact, I had simply evaded the possibility of ever having to make the choice. It is an illusion to suppose that a man can make a genuinely free decision about celibacy when, if he really intends to become a priest, the choice is already made. That is the fundamental reason why the present so-called education for celibacy in seminaries is not about educating for choice but about removing choice.

It is no answer to the charge that compulsory celibacy greatly damages the development of human personality by effectively denying freedom in a crucial area of being to say that no one is forced to become a priest: the Church authorities, after all, are not forced to couple priesthood to celibacy and it is a pity to give the impression of arrogantly trying to tie God's hands. The plain fact is that a law of this kind prevents a seminary student from objectively weighing up all the aspects and obligations of his vocation. His conviction that God is calling him to ministry will decide for him in advance that he is called to celibacy as well, simply because he knows that he will be committed

13

to celibacy if he is ordained. He cannot be said to exercise a truly free choice on the possibility of marriage for that is not an option.

Many Catholics, clerical and lay, nevertheless adamantly reject the charge of lack of freedom. They insist that any man who offers himself for ordination knows the rules: if he accepts ordination he knows he is accepting celibacy and should not want to change the rules afterwards just because he has met a girl he likes. Such conduct, they robustly maintain, smacks strongly of moral weakness. We should like such critics to reflect very seriously on what is being said here. This will help them to begin to understand that it is the very presence of the law which actually prevents the candidate from knowing the rules in any meaningful sense. When a person is sure in his mind that he is called by God's authority to ministry he is effectively disabled from giving any truly objective thought to the price demanded by the human authorities involved.

Because celibacy and ministry are coupled by Church authority and not by divine ordinance, serious psychological consequences can and do ensue. A young man aspiring to the priesthood, and even more so a boy (Church authority, as Pope John Paul II notes in his 1992 response to the 1990 Synod of Bishops on the priesthood, *Pastores Dabo Vobis*, still believes that junior seminaries can be a good idea), experiences great difficulty relating naturally and in ordinary freedom to a girl because of the danger that she might become a threat to his future priesthood. From the moment he seriously embarks upon the course leading to the priesthood, the issue of celibacy is settled for him; consequently, he has no genuinely free choice. Ironically, this has, by implication, been recognized by the

Church authorities. The Second Vatican Council's *Decree on Priestly Formation*, says approvingly that 'In minor seminaries, which are built to nurture the seeds of a vocation, students can be *conditioned* to follow Christ with a generous and pure heart' (Abbott, ed., *Documents of Vatican II*, p. 441).

'Conditioning' is certainly the right term. Spiritual writers and directors, confessors, older priests, the laity's expectations, the ecclesiastical system and the priest's own conscience all combine to portray women as a threat to what comes to be presented as a priest's chief quality: his chastity. Prudence, caution, circumspection, keeping a table between you and the Latin tags, *numquam solus cum sola januis clausis* and *noli tangere* ('Never be alone with a woman with the doors closed', 'do not touch'), are the outworks of the fortress of priestly purity. The priest faces a formidable task if he wishes to be a true pastor, bringing the love, sympathy and tenderness of Christ to both the men and the women who seek his help. And of course the effort to adhere to the rules aggravates the very tensions the rules are supposed to prevent.

Quite early in my pastoral ministry I made two illuminating discoveries. The first was that women are not, in fact, the moral threat supposed in the minds of the priestly spiritual experts: they are ordinary human beings, just like their male counterparts, with their own problems and difficulties, their own spiritual needs and their own desire to make sense of their Christian vocation in a hostile world. They do not appreciate being treated as part of the obstacle to Christian life when they seek the priest's help. The second was that ecclesiastical propaganda and policies can have a dangerous effect upon some Catholic women's perceptions, in that they are inclined to regard the priest as 'safe' in a way that they might not regard another unmarried man as 'safe'. The married clergymen of other churches (to whom, incidentally, Pope John Paul II pays scant courtesy in his regular insistence – for example, in *Pastores Dabo Vobis* – upon the bond between whole-hearted priestly devotion and sexual abstinence), like married male doctors and others in caring professions, achieve whatever maturity they possess from their experience of life which has been widened and deepened by their being married and by the need to cope with various economic pressures. That experience helps to make them, for the most part – there are, naturally, tragic exceptions – 'safe' counsellors. This is not, of course, to suggest that marriage automatically ensures maturity, wisdom and a balanced personality: we all know celibates who are fully rounded human beings of sound judgement and common sense, and married people notably lacking in these qualities. In general, however, there has been in the past a tendency among women to feel that the priest's vocation provided automatic protection from their mutual sexuality, often leading to intolerable strain on the one side and bitter disillusion on the other. I reflect now with embarrassment on the stiffness and awkwardness with which as a priest I treated many women, keeping not only them but their troubles at a distance so that there should be no sullying of what Pope Paul VI, in his encyclical letter *Sacerdotalis Caelibatus*, described with more optimism than accuracy as the Church's 'brilliant jewel'. I count it as one of the greatest graces of my life that finally sympathy proved stronger than safety and that I can now number several women among my closest and dearest friends. One of those, of course, became more than simply a friend.

My wife, Imelda, and I met in June 1964. She was on the staff of a Roman Catholic College of Education which was sited in the parish where I was curate. Ours was not a case of love at first sight. One factor in the development of our friendship was my gradual and humbling realization that engagement in pastoral care is a two-way process: it is an experience in which both are able to give and to receive, which of course is the essence of love. Another was the loving care which Imelda showed to my mother when she suffered a severe stroke. She gave up most of a summer vacation to nurse her at home. The circumstances inevitably threw us together in a rather more informal environment than would normally have occurred. They also heightened the tensions arising from our anxiety not to trespass on territory fenced off by the law of clerical celibacy.

Moralists will doubtless observe that once my mother was better and Imelda had returned to her own home we should have terminated our friendship, regardless of either her need or of the solid benefits – spiritual and psychological – which the friendship had certainly brought us. In terms of traditional Roman Catholic teaching the moralists are probably quite right. Whether they are right in terms of authentic Christian living is another matter. Human need is surely not to be pitched out of doors for the sake of ecclesiastical tidiness. Could it really, I asked myself, be God's will that the joy, strength and support which I was beginning to find in my friendship and burgeoning love for Imelda should be of less account than a law made by men who had no experience of the area for which they so blithely legislated?

A Priestless People?

The official policy of compulsory clerical celibacy in fact carries within it the seeds of its own destruction. This is the inevitable result of putting the main emphasis in priestly training on the preservation of celibacy. Students before and priests after ordination are constantly warned that the chief evil of spiritual laxity lies, not in the damage it might do to pastoral effectiveness, but in the threat which it is alleged to pose to celibacy. Of course, celibacy is presented as an aid to pastoral effectiveness and when I was ordained, I fully shared this outlook. I believed in the indissoluble union of priesthood and celibacy because I assumed that it conferred a freedom from the trammels of love which could not but be a positive hindrance to my ministry.

It was therefore a considerable shock to me – as I believe it is to many other men after ordination – when I finally admitted to myself that I did love Imelda, to discover that the official view was simply mistaken. Human love not only need not be any restraint on ministry, it can also be a positive aid to more effective ministry. Such claims are obviously open to the charge of wishful thinking. I was only too conscious of the probable reaction of some of my fellow clergy, especially those whose own fears and inhibitions required bolstering by the cynical imputation of unworthy motives to those priests who no longer felt that the Church's *law* of celibacy possessed validity in either reason or justice. I can only say that Imelda and I honestly testify that neither of us experienced any sense of alienation from God or any anxiety that our love was in itself creating obstacles to my pastoral work. These considerations made all the more hateful our realization of the necessity to keep our friendship secret; of course, we could not expect to be understood, let alone approved. I doubt

18

if our situation could have been understood, save by those in a similar situation – and they would themselves be in need of support and understanding.

Obviously, our position imposed a strain upon us both, and I steadily became more and more alienated from the clerical Church in which I had grown up and to whose service I had intended and still wished to devote my life. We experienced that it was simply not true that human love was, as we had all been taught, a rival to the love of God. Genuinely human love cannot be a competitor for God's love; if it is perceived to be so, it is properly neither human nor love. Assuredly, we found that through human love, God's love could be far better sensed and more deeply understood. Through our friendship we gained a deeper understanding of the meaning of love, of love for all our fellow human beings and for God, the source of all our loving. When many years later at London University I came to study the poems of John Donne, I understood what he meant when he wrote after the death of his wife:

> Here the admiring her my mind did whet
> To seek thee God; so streams do show the head.

Cardinal Heenan, Archbishop of Westminster from 1963 to 1975, once quoted with approval Francis Bacon's curious observation that 'A single life doth well with churchmen; for charity will hardly water the ground where it must first fill a pool'. This is exactly the misunderstanding of the nature of love to which the religious celibate is especially prone. Love is not a given quantity which is diminished by being spread. I found the intensity of one particular love made it easier, not harder, to love others;

it enabled me to make more, not less, sense of my prayers; it gave me greater, not less, conviction when I tried to speak to others of the depths of the love of God. But all this made the unhuman – indeed, as I saw with increasing clarity – *anti*-human character of the official Church more and more obvious. The insights gained from our friendship increasingly made me feel that to remain in the priesthood, as our Church leadership understood the term, was not merely to do violence to my own integrity but also, and more importantly, to be party to deceiving our people as to the true nature of the Christian life.

In the present state of the Church's official understanding of priesthood, if an individual priest no longer believes that the law of compulsory celibacy is an automatically beneficial aspect of his calling, he is assumed to have failed as a priest; celibacy has become the chief virtue of the priesthood with an essential role in preserving a quasi-magical view of its function. The priest must be a male, cultic figure, recognized as possessing sacred powers which set him apart from the ordinary faithful; no language describing him as a servant of the community can hide the fact that this is Rome's fundamental view. Ironically, the determination of the present Pope to ensure that as few priests as possible leave the priesthood, and that those who do so will only rarely be dispensed from their clerical obligations, is producing a situation – graphically illustrated in 1992 in the tragic personal history of the former Bishop of Galway and in more recent episcopal tragedies since – in which celibacy is, in practice, more important than chastity.

Behind this attitude there seems to be a philosophy of life and a theology of the Incarnation which regards being human with all that it entails – physically, emotionally, sexually, intellectually, maleness and femaleness – with suspicion, if not actual fear and dislike. The maintenance of an all-male, celibate priesthood is the essential expression of this outlook. Once any individual priest has experienced that a belief in compulsory celibacy is not at all necessary to effective ministry and that, indeed, it may hinder it, that a relationship with a woman is not identical with a preoccupation with physical sex, and that in fact it is the celibate hierarchy who are the ones obsessed with sex, then a profound change comes over his attitude to the Church and his role within it. He can truly say that he did not so much leave the priesthood in order to marry as that the desire to marry flowered in a new vision of priesthood; such a realization is blocked by the present blinkered discipline of the Church.

3

Catholic Upbringing: A Personal Account

> ... always have your answer ready for people who ask you for the reason for the hope that you have.
>
> *(1 Peter 3:15)*

Many Catholics, both clerical and lay, attempt to rebut the criticism that official Church policy is partly responsible for the vocations crisis by suggesting that the priests who leave and the women who marry them must have been unsatisfactory and dissatisfied members of the Church from the start. Some such notion clearly lies behind current official ecclesiastical policy towards priests who wish to leave the ordained ministry. Under Pope John Paul II, a priest has little chance of receiving official permission to resign unless he either has a wife and children dependent upon him (the absence of such impedimenta will, in the unlikely event of his being given a dispensation, cruelly leave the celibacy obligation intact) or can prove that his ordination was invalid on account of some inadequacy in himself which the seminary authorities failed to detect. Either condition requires the admission of guilt and/or failure on the part of the priest. This approach fails to take into account the possibility that the decision to leave the form of active ministry demanded by human ecclesiastical authority is not, in fact, destructive of the original commitment to service; it may be the priest's understanding of the reality to which he is committed which has changed. It is even possible that the current conception of priesthood is itself one of the factors contributing to a priest's 'defection', which is the morally loaded term describing a priest's resignation. This account of my wife's and my own backgrounds should help to balance and to modify the judgement which attributes all priestly defection to priestly defect.

My own background could scarcely have been more orthodox. It was one which was closely bound up with the institutional life of the Church. The Church was quite simply part of the general routine and, indeed, security of my life, like going to school, shopping for my mother in the Co-op and spending summer holidays with my relatives in Scotland. It was serving the 7.45 a.m. Mass (all Masses were a.m. in those days) on weekdays and the 9.15 with my brother on Sundays, having first of all been to Communion before the 8 o'clock Mass, because I was sick if I fasted from midnight (as we had to do then before Communion) until after the 9.15 Mass. It was Benediction on Sunday afternoons and going home with my parents' friends afterwards, hoping that one of them would be a particular Irish lady who seemed to have an inexhaustible fund of wonderful stories. It was, too, confession every fortnight and the sense of relief provided by those occasions when I was genuinely aware that I had actually committed a recognizable and nameable sin at least once, so that there would be something definite to tell the priest. The priest

was usually our kindly, sympathetic and wholly approach-
able parish priest. He was Church too. My family were on
very close terms with him. He was a frequent visitor to
our home and became friend, adviser and mentor to my
brother and myself. He relied entirely on my father not only
to stoke and manage the church's temperamental boiler but
also to repair it, together with all the other contemporary
technological equipment in the 1914 ex-army hut which
served as a makeshift church in our village right down to
the 1950s. Our entire social life was one with the life of
the parish.

We were firmly and serenely members of the one, holy,
catholic and apostolic true Church of Christ. We did not
in those days call ourselves *Roman* Catholics because that
might have implied a concession to those members of the
Church of England who also laid claim to the title, albeit
with the qualifying prefix 'English' or 'Anglo'. We were
aware of people who were not Catholics; some of the non-
Catholic children called us Roman candles, but we felt glad
to suffer something for the faith from these 'proddy dogs',
which was, I am sorry to say, our term for our Protestant
brothers and sisters. But they made no real impact on our
lives, which moved in a tight circle in which we went to
Mass, Rosary and Benediction, said our prayers, confessed
our sins, invited to tea the parish priest and the nuns evacuated from London (my father was their odd-job man too,
breaking into their bungalow when they forgot their key
and removing the oven door to provide access for the
Christmas turkey), and stayed happy in our little closed
world.

It was the Catholic school – I always went to Catholic
schools save for one bewildering fortnight in the alien land

of the local State primary – which first made me aware of what in later, more learned, years I came to call ecclesiology. In the Sixth Form, I was introduced to Sheehan's *Apologetics and Catholic Doctrine*, M. H. Gill & Son Ltd, Dublin. For the first time I learned that not only was Catholicism true, it could also, apparently, be *proved* to be true. With great enthusiasm, I set about 'converting' my few non-Catholic friends. I was rather surprised that not only did they not eagerly accept the comprehensive proofs which I offered, they were not even interested in the question. I left school in 1949 without a convert to my name.

Nonetheless, when I started work, with more determination than discernment I set about witnessing to the faith and was often involved in religious discussions. We had the Truth; I was bent on ensuring that others should have it too. It was all part of our total, absolute, religious certainty. I still recall my puzzlement at the indignant reaction of one of my office colleagues when, to his question about the Catholic view of the fate of those who refused to accept our Church's assessment of its unique role in Christian mission, I comfortingly answered that God accepts their good faith because they are mostly invincibly ignorant. The state of 'invincible ignorance' was the theologians' solution to the difficulty posed to Catholic exclusivism by the fact that the majority of the human race was either ignorant of or rejected its teaching. It was not a solution which would have appealed to Pope Boniface VIII or to the Council of Florence (1438–45). Boniface VIII decreed that 'we declare, state, define and pronounce that, for salvation, it is entirely necessary that every human creature be subject to the Roman Pontiff' (Declaration 469, quoted in Denzinger, *Enchiridion Symbolorum*, p. 220, Herder);

the Council of Florence, called to restore unity between the Roman Catholic Church and the Greek Orthodox Church, laid down as one of the conditions for that reunion the following:

> The Holy Roman Church, founded by the voice of our Lord and Saviour, firmly believes, professes and preaches that no one not actually existing within the Catholic Church – and this includes not simply pagans, but also Jews or heretics and schismatics – can share in eternal life, but will go to the eternal fire which was prepared for the devil and his angels, unless they are brought into that Church before the end of their lives. So important is the unity of the body of the Church, that the sacraments of the Church profit for salvation only those who remain in it; and likewise, the fasting, almsgiving and other works and exercises of devotion performed in the church militant, bring forth the reward of eternal life (only for those remaining in the church). No one can be saved, no matter how great his almsdeeds, even if he were to shed his blood for Christ, unless he remains within the womb and unity of the Catholic Church.
>
> (Declaration 714, Denzinger, op. cit., p. 265.)

I certainly brought no doubts to my membership of the Catholic Evidence Guild, which I joined in 1950. At street corners in Putney, Brixton and South Croydon, on the common at Streatham and in the market place which used to exist outside Waterloo, I proclaimed the faith and the proofs which went with it, quoting to what I am sure now was a totally uncomprehending audience the Fathers of the

Catholic Upbringing: A Personal Account

Church and Carlyle's ecclesiastical history. Fortified by the certainties of the Australian lay theologian and publisher Frank Sheed's book, *Theology and Sanity*, Sheed & Ward, 1947, and the polemics of the mountaineering convert Arnold Lunn, I welcomed and answered objections to and queries on the entire spectrum of Church history and dogma. Our great inspiration at that time was Pope Pius XII. He embodied this self-confident, all-embracing, absolutist attitude. We were glad to belong to a Church so strong, so sure and so unshakeable. All this was the stuff of the faith of our fathers, which we were genuinely and sincerely sure would be our faith and our children's and our children's children's faith to the end of time.

In that spirit of certainty I came at the age of twenty-one as a student for the priesthood to St John's, the Southwark diocesan seminary in the village of Wonersh near Guildford in Surrey. Did I have a true vocation to the priesthood? I certainly thought I had. My parish priest had tried very hard to ensure that I had. At the end of my School Certificate year at the Salesian College, Chertsey, I had become convinced that I had a vocation to the Salesians and in September 1947 I went off blithely to their junior seminary at Pott Shrigley in Cheshire. A further six weeks in the mist and rain from the western slopes of the Derbyshire Pennines, coupled with the effect of a boarding-school regime on a 14-year-old who had never before been away from home, cured me of the illusion that I had a vocation to the Salesians. But I was still sure that I had a vocation to the *priesthood*. That conviction sustained me through two years in the Sixth Form of St George's College, Weybridge, two years of national service and three years of work for the Borough of Woking (whose Anglican Town

Clerk concluded that I certainly had a vocation after he found me reading Newman's *Apologia Pro Vita Sua* during a slack period of duty as a polling clerk one election day in 1949!).

Nothing occurred during those six years to shake my belief that I was called by God to the priesthood or to make me fear that one day I too might be among those to be referred to in hushed tones as 'fallen priests'.

My wife's background was little different, but I had better let her tell her own story.

For me, too, life revolved around the local Catholic church and Catholic school, attending Mass and Benediction, joining the Catholic Youth Club and sharing in all the social activities of which there was a profusion. Life, therefore, was a tight circle of Catholic friends from school and church. At the beginning of the war we were evacuated first to Scotland and then to York. Ironically the title 'Catholic' which in one sense means 'open to everyone' failed to live up to its name when I attended school there; I was very unhappy feeling unaccepted, probably because I spoke differently from all the other children. I remember feeling frightened and threatened much of the time. I missed the family atmosphere and individual care of the small Catholic primary school I attended at home and longed to return there.

My initiation into active sacramental life was telescoped because of war conditions. I made my first confession, and first Holy Communion and was confirmed all in the same year, aged seven. Looking back, I wonder what I was promising at Confirmation; my only recollection of the ceremony is that the bishop was very tall.

At 11 years of age I went to the local convent grammar school where we were taught the faith with all its certainties. Study of scripture was not detailed but highly selective in order to prove the authenticity of our faith and I can recall little questioning of what we were taught. My taking issue with our nun-teacher's statement that illegitimacy was a bar to religious profession, on the grounds that God would not be so discriminatory, was viewed askance. In the last year of school we studied Apologetics, the science of the defence of the faith. I think I remember being told that God could not make a square circle, but little else. Our minds were filled at that time with revision for the Religious Teacher's Examination for those of us wishing to enter Catholic Colleges of Higher Education.

At 18 I went to La Sainte Union Teachers' Training College (now College of Higher Education) in Southampton. My conventional Catholic upbringing left me at any rate – some of my friends were more adventurous – perfectly happy with the semi-convent character of college life, epitomized in the grave warning not to go at night below 'Bar' – the Bar Gate leading to Southampton Docks. Nevertheless, I spent two very happy years there studying hard in the secure environment of another Catholic institution.

At Southampton my main course of study was Geography, and I also took an advanced course in Religious Education as I was one of the students intending to teach in secondary/grammar schools. During subsequent years I undertook two supplementary courses: one in Physical Education (now known as Movement Studies) at

St Gabriel's College, Camberwell, and the other in Ceramics at the College of Art and Design. These two courses were my first experience of studying outside my Catholic environment, and I found myself for the first time in a different world.

After completing the course, I taught for the next four years in Catholic primary, secondary modern and grammar schools. None of my study – and Religious Education played a very important part in it – was to prepare me adequately for what I was to find in the 'real world'. Teaching in Catholic schools raised no theological doubts at first in my then unenquiring mind. My main subject was PE combined with Health Education, and in that capacity I was judged suitable also to teach RE both to my own and the top form. The syllabus for the final year was the study of Pope Pius XI's Encyclical on marriage, *Casti Conubii*. To teach this, I obtained books and information from the local priest. Our contribution to my pupils' understanding on the subject must have been severely limited since I was still single and the priest committed to celibacy. What I was teaching would in any case have been very difficult for my pupils to understand since a large proportion of them had been abandoned by their parents and were in local authority care. It was simply a case of teaching what we had been taught to teach. I do, however, remember, when called upon to teach RE to a group of non-Catholic children in the grammar school, being surprised to discover that some children did not believe in such things as the visions at Fatima.

Gradually, however, and almost imperceptibly, I detected a growing number of unanswered questions about some of the Church's moral teachings as I came up against such social problems as broken homes and children in care: stern ecclesiastical admonitions about the permanence of marriage and the immorality of second marriages seemed increasingly remote from the reality of daily life.

I remained deeply involved in parish life. I did much of the secretarial work, helped with the parish census and acted as unofficial chauffeur to the parish priest. Our home, too, remained a place of refuge for priests in difficulties of one kind or another. My mother always had a bed and a meal for those with nowhere to go, and several of those were priests – apart, of course, from the many relatives and friends who came for visits and holidays of varying length. It used to be a happy joke in the family that it was a good idea to go to bed early to make sure of getting one! One of my sisters has spent, I think, more nights out of her own bed than in, because this early way of life has continued into her adulthood – her home is a constant refuge for the broken-limbed and the broken-hearted, animal and human alike.

At the end of those four years, I was fortunate enough to be appointed to the staff of a Catholic College of Education. Here I continued to lecture in PE and Health Education, but the problems of the real world began to impinge increasingly upon my consciousness. As the years passed, more and more students came to me with their personal difficulties, many of which were deeply bound up with official Church teaching on sex, marriage and religious vocation. Some of the mature students had already experienced the trauma of separation or divorce and I found growing difficulty in reconciling official doctrine and policy with the day-to-day needs, anxieties and actual suffering of so many of my students. Added to this was the growing influence of the spirit of Vatican II on the life of the college, particularly in the liturgy. The new, young chaplain made a real effort to implement the decrees of the Council and I became increasingly aware of the growing gap between college and parish church life. This in turn stimulated further thought and reading, encouraged, I have to say, by what I heard Vincent say in his sermons at the local parish church. For both of us, although we did not know one another well at that time, it was not a predisposition to rebellion but our experience of the actual world in which men and women lived, loved, suffered and died which carried us further and further from the simplistic Church of our youth.

4

The Training of Priests

How can any man who does not understand how
to manage his own household take care of the
Church of God?

(1 Timothy 3:5)

There can be little doubt that the style of training for the
priesthood which prevailed in pre-Vatican II days has
much to do with the departure of so many priests from
that era. My own course was certainly not one calculated
to spur much inner questioning. Great care was taken in
the first place to maintain the seminary as, in the spiritual
writers' phrase, a *'hortus conclusus'*, a walled garden.
Exposure to the world which we were supposedly being
trained to serve was carefully screened by a network of
rules, which ranged from a ban on speaking to the domestic
staff to the requirement that students should go out on
foot and only in groups of three or four, of whom at
least one must have commenced his theology course which
began in the third year. In practice, groups of four were
frowned upon owing to the danger of splitting into two
pairs with all the dangers which the seminary authorities
were certain would result from the particular friendships
which would inevitably be produced. The rules also
explicitly prescribed that students on walks must have a

hat. Since those same rules did not specifically state that the hat be actually worn, the budding canon lawyers among us decided, without rebuke from authority, that the demands of the law could be met if the hats of the group were placed in one bag to be carried in turn by each member. From such materials was the metal of our priesthood forged.

The intellectual content of the course was not particularly taxing. A student who consulted the Church history professor about a particular difficulty was told to concentrate on more important matters. A moral theology examination once asked us to state the number of sins committed by an Irish labourer working on a Sunday on a building site for an Anglican church, and to give our views on the validity of an absolution given by a curate to a nun who made her confession to him while they were both swimming in the local bathing pool. Regurgitation of received instruction was the criterion for success and those students who distinguished themselves in such examinations were gravely warned against contracting spiritual pride.

Yet, discussion of theological issues was not entirely absent. In my last year, with the rector's nervous consent, we held a debate on birth control in which I spoke vigorously in defence of the official teaching.

Prizes, surely a scandal in any educational enterprise and doubly so in ecclesiastical education, were awarded to the students who came first in the various examinations. Their cash value indicated the degree of regard in which the subjects were held. Dogma came top at £5, with moral theology a close second at £4. Canon law came next at, I think, £3. I won this twice, an achievement which I pray will be forgiven me at the Last Judgement. Church history was discounted at 27/6 (£1.375) and shared with sacred scripture the distinction of receiving the least amount of time in the curriculum. The sacred scripture prize was awarded for the best (voluntary) essay, a competition which excited little interest. But at least scripture was a compulsory subject during my training: not so long before, it had been optional. I read books on Church history avidly during the two weekly lectures allocated to that discipline, which consisted simply of readings from the professor's own notes, but we emerged from the scripture course with no desire to read further in the Bible. Priority was given to declarations from Rome. Little time was devoted to showing how those declarations were arrived at. They were, moreover, presented to us as an entirely consistent logical development over the centuries. A more thorough presentation of Church history would have given us a more balanced view.

Great importance was attached to what our superiors sincerely conceived to be our spiritual formation. This, it was quite properly hoped, would be achieved at least partly by regular religious exercises. These began, after rising at 6 o'clock, with half an hour's meditation together in chapel. Bodily posture was decided by the Rector's preferences for kneeling or sitting. Mass followed at 7 o'clock, accompanied in October by five decades of the Rosary, pausing only for the consecration. At midday there was an exercise called 'Particular Examen', whose precise purpose and value I never discovered. After lunch, the whole community of staff and students made a private 'visit' to the Blessed Sacrament and a public one (that is, with public set prayers) around 3 o'clock after compulsory outdoor exercise. At 7 p.m. there was either 'Spiritual Reading' conducted privately together in the chapel or, in a lecture room, the reading of and commentary from the Rector upon the Rule, the seminarian's comprehensive guide – if not to heaven, at any rate to ordination. The day closed with public night prayers at nine, followed by the 'Grand Silence' with lights out at 9.30. Deacons were permitted to read until 10.00 p.m. provided they read 'spiritual' books; Newman's *Grammar of Assent*, I was firmly told, was *not* spiritual reading. Deacons were also able to enrich their spiritual diet through the daily recitation of the Divine Office – in Latin, of course – during which they were allowed the privilege of doffing the biretta otherwise required to be worn at all times.

Connected with this spiritual formation and with a desire both to widen our cultural horizons and to improve our elocution, lunch on most days was accompanied by public reading in the refectory. The reading and the meal always concluded with the day's passage from the *Roman Martyrology*, and woe betide the overconfident reader who, thinking from daily hearing that he knew the concluding phrases '*et alibi aliorum*', etc., by heart, closed the book too soon and found himself embroiled in a tongue-twisting mesh of ill-remembered sentences. Such reading sessions were occasionally enlivened by errors by students, one of whom thought that the pronunciation of a night watchman's brazier, at which his fellow workmen were warming their hands, was the same as for a female support garment, and another who, announcing the altar servers for the week, misread the Latin title '*admodum*' for our not undernourished Rector as 'abdomen'.

Even odder than this enforcement of a monastic regime on men who were going to live in and minister to a secular world in which they would have to organize and take responsibility for their own lives was the fact that few of us found it odd. Most of us, I suspect, enjoyed the regularity and security of the routine which provided immunity from real problems and created the illusion that we were daily coming closer to God. It was a system which fostered narcissism: lost in the contemplation of our own navels, we had neither time nor disposition to look to the community aspect of the Church or to the responsibility of Christians for our whole world. Preoccupied with polishing our souls, we had little concrete awareness either of Christianity as an incarnational religion or that if ministry is to mean anything, it must mean ministry to flesh-and-blood human beings who for the most part, even in comfortable parishes, were leading lives of far greater strain, effort and sacrifice than we were likely to experience. A great deal was said about *prayer* in the seminary and a large portion of the timetable was allocated to it; I do not think we learned much about *praying*. We learned even less about the God of our prayer as revealed in the *humanity* of Jesus, our suffering, dying and loving Lord. Humanness was largely spiritualized out of a consciousness encased throughout our waking hours in black cassock and biretta.

Some students were certainly unhappy with the system. They disliked the pettiness of the rules, the restrictive atmosphere, the curb on open access to the world. Two newspapers were supplied for the entire 100-plus student body, *The Times* and the *Daily Telegraph*, and even these were occasionally censored, though for moral not political reasons. The radio was available for only half an hour each evening in the lower common room, known as 'The Dive'. Some students endured the six years of Wonersh simply as a means to the desired end of priesthood. But I do not think theirs was the general attitude. Most of us were happy in our well-fed, comfortable, material and spiritual security in which we, unlike so many of our contemporaries in the world, did not have to struggle to make our way in life.

None of this is intended to suggest that there was nothing good about the seminary course. Our professors were all devoted priests and certainly had no other aim than to produce more good and holy priests for the service of the Church. The great defect of the system, in addition to the disastrous inadequacy of its theology, was that it bred in us a far too individualistic, introverted and non-human conception of the meaning of holiness. It has been said that the problem with Protestants is that they love their neighbour without loving God and with Catholics that they love God without loving their neighbour. The partial truth of the epigram illustrates the flaw in our training. A God in heaven, not the incarnational God revealed in Jesus Christ, was to be the centre of our lives; and people were to be important not for themselves but as objects upon which we could exercise our love for God. It is admittedly only too easy to criticize, even to ridicule, the seminary training of the 1950s from the superior standpoint of the post-Vatican II Church. Yet, I do not believe that the criticisms are unjust. Those who feel that they are must convincingly explain the mass exodus of priests since Vatican II, many declared by their people to be among the most intelligent, the most dedicated and the holiest, and the continuing complaint from all parts of the Church that so many priests who remain offer little vision or mature inspiration and leadership in the day-to-day struggle to lead truly Christian lives.

The Training of Priests

Can we look forward to a better future for the Church with the ordination of the students who are studying for the priesthood in the new seminaries? It is true that great efforts have been made in parts of the Church drastically to reform seminary training. My own seminary of St John's exemplifies the new approach. My wife and I are grateful to Bishop Peter Smith for allowing us, when he was Rector of the seminary, to spend a day there to experience the new-look approach. Gone, for instance, is the old system of a single interview for each candidate with the diocesan bishop and a few selected priests before admission. A male Catholic who feels he has a vocation to the priesthood is now first interviewed by the diocesan Vocations Director, a priest chosen for his pastoral experience, intellectual ability and proven loyalty to Church authority.

The candidate then attends a weekend selection conference at the seminary. During this weekend he is interviewed by a three-person team consisting of a priest, a layman and a laywoman. The priest's task is to assess spiritual suitability for the priesthood: this is judged by his sensitivity to spiritual matters, the quality and depth of his faith and his potential for apostolic work. It is obviously not expected that the candidate will have reached the required standard at this stage, but only that there will be evidence of, in the words of the seminary prospectus, 'the character, stability, stamina and moral rectitude, which will be a good foundation for preparation for the priesthood'. The lay male interviewer is usually someone from the educational world who assesses the candidate's intellectual development and capacity; the laywoman, often someone with experience of counselling, assesses his ability to form relationships against the background of his home and past social experience. Clearly, these three areas cannot be kept in watertight compartments and it is hoped that the inevitable overlapping will help form a more complete picture.

The candidates gather for a group discussion at which are also present a psychiatrist and two of the seminary students to facilitate the discussion. The purpose of this exercise is to test the candidates' ability to relate to members of a group and the psychiatrist grades each of them. A psychological assessment and a physical medical report also have to be drawn up. There is, in addition, a purely social gathering which existing seminary students attend. Their impressions are taken into consideration in the interviewing panel's assessment of the candidates' ability to fit into seminary life. That the students' judgements normally coincide with the interviewers' is hardly surprising since those same students will themselves have been selected in accordance with the interviewers' criteria.

When the weekend is over, the members of the interviewing teams meet to discuss their findings and to make their own final assessments. This is followed by a further meeting of the seminary Rector, a psychiatrist, a psychologist and a medical doctor to sift out any major problems. Finally, there is a plenary session in which final recommendations are prepared for submission to the candidates' individual bishops. It is the bishop who makes the final decision whether to accept the candidate for training for the priesthood.

Clearly, this is a far more thorough selection procedure than was prevalent when I offered myself as a candidate in 1954. At that time, the greatest weight was given to the parish priest's report and a successful physical medical examination which required, among other matters, a testimony from the doctor that all the candidate's limbs were perfect.

Serious questions nevertheless remain to be answered. No one would wish to deny, though many undoubtedly regret, that today's Catholic Church exhibits an unprecedented degree of controversy across an astonishingly broad theological and disciplinary spectrum. Many of the issues, for example, the ordination of women, the place of women in the Church, compulsory celibacy, the nature of a sacrament, the Gospel interpretation of authority, etc., affect our understanding of the nature, status and function of priesthood in the Church. The present Church leadership, at almost every level, refuses to heed – let alone discuss – alternative strategies and approaches to ministry and Church discipline and doctrine which diverge from an established narrow base demanded by the authorities in Rome. It is inevitable, therefore, that those chosen to administer the selection procedures represent only one particular strand of theological opinion and pastoral expectation in the Church. It would be good to know precisely the criteria for the appointment of members of interviewing panels, both clerical and lay, and the willingness of those appointed to take account of the full breadth of reputable theological and ecclesiological opinion in the Church, even where it may differ from that favoured by authority. To ignore this aspect of the life of the Church community is to increase the vulnerability of candidacy for the priesthood to the already frequent charge of insensitivity to many of the real difficulties and needs of the Church in today's world.

The academic training does not appear, in essence, to differ greatly from that of my own day, except that it is now largely concentrated in the first five years of the course. While study is not excluded from the sixth year, a large proportion of that year consists of full-time practical pastoral work as a deacon in a parish. The academic study covers the usual ground of scripture, philosophy, Church history, canon law, liturgy and theology. In moral theology and canon law, particular attention is paid to the study of marriage, human sexuality and bioethics within what is called the evolving tradition of the Church; this is complemented in the deacons' pre-ordination short course by a further study of medical ethics. The students' own ability to communicate is cultivated through professional guidance on public speaking and reading with practice in year five in preaching. The effort is made to develop counselling skills through a course in the theology of pastoral care.

A potentially exciting new development has been the provision of an opportunity for some of the students to study for the Bachelor of Theology Degree awarded by Southampton University. Since the course provided by the seminary must be validated by the University, this has had the effect of providing Wonersh with an excellent theological library which reflects a wide spectrum of theological opinion. The students' general academic progress is monitored by a system of continuous assessment and formal examination, both written and oral.

It is clear that on paper the content of the course is both demanding and substantial. It is not so clear that its intellectual ambitions are widely fulfilled. It is alarming for the future theological life of the Church that it is by no means the overwhelming majority of the students who qualify to take the theology degree course. It is difficult to escape the impression that considerations of personal piety

and goodness weigh more heavily than intellectual potential. Clearly a priesthood bereft of holiness can contribute
little to the promotion of the reign of God, but holiness is
ordinarily no substitute for well-founded knowledge and
wisdom in the ordering of human affairs according to the
mind of God. St Teresa of Avila is credited with the observation that, had she to choose between a holy and an
intelligent spiritual director, she would choose the latter:
in general, the principle should hold good for training for
the pastoral ministry. Regretfully but honestly we have to
say that we have been able to discern among either students
or priests little evidence of that spirit of searching enquiry,
scholarly rigour and intellectual excitement which are the
authentic characteristics of the genuinely academic institution. The average student in our secular universities does
not habitually exhibit a grave demeanour and a professorial stoop, but she/he is generally enthusiastic about
her/his chosen discipline and anxious to sharpen the mind
and develop the understanding. Is this the impression
created by the average seminary student either before or
after ordination?

Equally disturbing is the question of intellectual freedom. It jars when talking with seminary students to be
asked not to be quoted. The request is often made with a
laugh to suggest that it is not really serious, but it is difficult
not to detect beneath the outwardly lighthearted manner
a real fear that free speech and admission to orders will
be seen as incompatible ingredients of a priestly vocation.
One seminary moral theology professor, explicitly proud
of his total loyalty to the official Roman line in ethical
questions, made his attitude quite clear. He told us that,
although the secular university authorities may judge the

quality of a paper purely by the cogency of the candidate's reasoning, he reminds his students that doctrinal conformity is the more important consideration in assessing their suitability for ordination. While even the most liberal Catholic would surely accept that our seminaries ought not to be breeding grounds for heresy, all Catholics ought to be alarmed that deacons approaching their final examinations clearly feel that it would not be prudent to reveal to authority their personal opinions on disputed questions. Priests above all cannot, and should not try to, live lives in which private conviction is at variance with public proclamation. The inevitable outcome will be not only personally destructive to the priest but also highly damaging to the public authority and good name of the Church. Rashly to publish to the world ill-thought out conclusions is clearly no service to the People of God, but failure to bear witness to a sincere and well-founded personal conviction will equally ill serve a community whose Lord promised it the guidance of the Spirit into *all* truth. The Church's leadership has yet to find a means of accommodating differences of opinion in areas of Church teaching not definitively settled. The refusal to do so has already dealt the Church severe wounds; and these will not be healed by describing as 'development of doctrine' the adoption by present and future authority of positions condemned by that same authority in the past.

Sadly, all the present signs are that Church authority is becoming less understanding of dissent. Pope John Paul II's Encyclical, *Veritatis Splendor*, declares that 'Opposition to the teaching of the Church's Pastors cannot be seen as a legitimate expression of either Christian freedom or of the diversity of the Spirit's gifts' (§113). Ominously, it warns that bishops must 'have recourse to appropriate measures to ensure that the faithful are guarded from every doctrine and theory contrary to it, that is the Word of God as interpreted by the magisterium' (§116).

Members of the Church ought also to be concerned at some aspects of the teaching given to students on the nature of the priesthood. It is, of course, a commonplace of Catholic understanding of priesthood that the priest be regarded as *alter Christus*, another Christ. In the past, however, and certainly when I was a seminary student, this description implied a distinctly limited identification with Christ. Just as, according to the theology of the day, Jesus had consecrated bread and wine as his body and blood and absolved from sin, so the priest too had 'power' to consecrate and to absolve. It was expected, too, that the priest would make a special effort to build into his life the love, generosity, spirit of service and self-sacrifice which were characteristic of the Lord he served. Current seminary theological teaching seems to go dangerously beyond these ideas. Much emphasis is laid on a conception of priesthood which involves some kind of assimilation of the human priest to the very person and nature of Christ. An article in the May 1992 issue of *Priests and People* exemplifies this approach:

The priest does the things that he [Jesus] does – above all presiding at the Eucharist, absolving sinners, anointing the sick, proclaiming and explaining the Good News with authority, giving blessings, and his general leadership of the local community of believers – because of what he became at his ordination: the sacramental sign of Jesus as shepherd and head of his Church. Jesus

exercises his own invisible leadership of his disciples
through the visible ministry of his priests.

(Michael Evans, *Priesthood: Something Worth
the Sacrifice*, p. 181.)

It is not difficult to see how this kind of language both
inflates the priest's sense of his importance to God's saving
plan for the world and diminishes the role of the laity. One
deacon, a few weeks away from ordination, with whom we
discussed this theology of the priesthood, seemed genuinely
surprised by the idea that all Christians, in virtue of their
baptism, are called to be 'other Christs'. There is a very
real danger in current seminary training on priesthood that
what should be the mission of the whole Church will
become – despite the plain statements of Vatican II, to say
nothing of the New Testament – even more the preserve
of the clergy. Pope John Paul II's insistence on the one
hand upon the essential function of the laity is contradicted
on the other by popular misinterpretation of his declaration in *Pastores Dabo Vobis* that 'priests exist and act in
order to proclaim the Gospel to the world'. Lay people
will never be persuaded of the reality of their share in the
priesthood of Christ so long as seminaries exaggerate the
papal teaching that 'Priests . . . are placed in the forefront
of the Church as signs of the presence of Christ' (quoted
in *The Tablet*, 18/25 April 1992, p. 526).

Although the twelfth-century law of clerical celibacy has
always encountered criticism and resistance, recent years
have seen their unprecedented intensification. The criticism
has been fuelled by an increasing number of public scandals
involving not only women, but paternity cases and charges
of child abuse. The seminary course reflects the Church

authority's increasing anxiety at these developments to such a degree that it is difficult to resist the impression that the underlying, principal aim of the course is either to ensure that the candidate does not leave to marry soon after ordination, or to be able to lay the fault entirely at his own door if he does so. It is no exaggeration to describe the effort to couple celibacy with priesthood in the student's mind as indoctrination. The always questionable assertion that priests freely choose celibacy is now a patent absurdity; the whole thrust of seminary training is to brainwash the student out of any free consideration of the question if he is to be taken seriously about wishing to be a priest. The Church authority's own doubts about the inner freedom of the candidate over both his professed orthodoxy and acceptance of the celibacy law are manifest in its requirement that he accept both under oath. According to Matthew 5:34–37, Jesus bids us

> do not swear at all, either by heaven, since that is God's throne; or by earth, since that is his footstool; or by Jerusalem, since that is the city of the great King. Do not swear by your own head either, since you cannot turn a single hair white or black. All you need say is 'Yes' if you mean yes, 'No' if you mean no; anything more than this comes from the Evil One.

Ecclesiastical authority, however, demands that the candidate declare on oath that 'I believe and profess, with a firm faith, each and all the articles which are contained in the Creed . . .', and there follows the text of the Nicene Creed. Attached to the Creed is the following affirmation:

Furthermore, I embrace and uphold each and every doctrine concerning faith and morals which the Church has taught and declared in solemn definition or by ordinary teaching authority – and in the sense in which the Church has proposed such doctrine – especially the teaching concerning the mystery of the Holy Church of Christ, the Sacraments, the Sacrifice of the Mass and the primacy of the Roman Pontiff.

It is not hard to see authority's anxieties lurking behind every word of this final affirmation. Such anxieties, of course, are far more evident – and far more frightening in their implications for Rome's understanding of the Church – in the new oath which the Vatican demanded with effect from 1 March 1989. From that date, vicars general, parish priests, rectors and professors of theology and philosophy in seminaries, rectors of ecclesiastical or Catholic universities, those who in any university teach subjects which deal with faith or morals, and those to be made deacons are required to make the following commitment: they must swear to fulfil their office 'with great diligence and fidelity', to 'preserve the whole deposit of the faith', to 'pass it on and explain it faithfully', and to avoid contrary teachings; 'to follow the discipline common to the Church' and to obey canon law; and to 'follow with Christian obedience those things' stated by the teachers and leaders of the Church and to assist diocesan bishops so that 'all proceed in communion with the Church'. Three new sentences have also been added to the standard profession of faith:

With a firm faith I also believe all those things which are contained in the word of God, whether written or handed on, and those things which are to be believed as proposed by the Church whether by a solemn judgement or by the ordinary and universal magisterium as divinely revealed.

I also firmly embrace and retain all and everything which is definitely proposed in doctrine either about faith or morals by the Church.

In addition I adhere by religious assent of the will and intellect to the teachings which either the Roman pontiff or the college of bishops declare when they exercise the authentic magisterium, *even if they do not intend to proclaim them by a definitive act.*

(My italics. See *The Tablet*, 11 March 1989, p. 289.)

Such an oath clearly aims seriously to curb intellectual freedom in the Church, to transform theological research into a defence structure and to reduce the theologian's role to a uniform exposition of the current Vatican interpretation of revelation. That this is the mind of authority is made clear in *Veritatis Splendor*, §110:

While recognizing the possible limitations of the human arguments employed by the Magisterium, moral theologians are called to develop a deeper understanding of the reasons underlying its teachings and to expound the validity and obligatory nature of the precepts it proposes, demonstrating their connection with one another and their relation with man's [sic] ultimate end. Moral theologians are to set forth the Church's teaching and to give, in the exercise of their ministry, the example of a loyal assent, both internal and external, to the

Magisterium's teachings in the areas of both dogma and morality.

The approach comes perilously near to the notorious Communist assertion that truth is identical with whatever serves the needs of the party at any given moment in history. The spirit of enquiry and a deepening understanding of the faith committed to the Church are to be sacrificed on the altar of authoritarian ecclesiastical convenience. Little wonder, then, that seminaries, for all the reforms in terms of freedom of dress, movement and – within limits – activity since the 1950s, remain intellectually oppressive institutions, by their very nature discouraging to enquirer and researcher alike.

The same note of fear pervades the 'Declaration of Freedom' to be made before the reception of each of the Major Orders (diaconate and priesthood) which, in accordance with Canon 1036 of the Church's Code of Canon Law, has to be written out by the candidate in his own handwriting and sworn to on the Gospels. Not only the concept of the document as a whole, but some of its individual propositions will astonish many readers.

I, the undersigned . . . . have already presented to the Bishop my petition for ordination to the (diaconate/priesthood). Now that the Ordination is near, I hereby testify and swear, after diligent consideration in the sight of God:

Firstly, that in receiving this Order I am in no way driven by coercion or force or by any fear; but that I desire it eagerly and of my own accord, and wish for it with full freedom of will, since I know clearly and realize that I am truly called by God.

And I affirm that I am fully aware of all the duties and responsibilities that are attached to this sacred Order; of my own free will I wish and intend to undertake these, and I am determined, with the help of God, to observe these most faithfully throughout my whole life.

In particular I declare that I am fully aware of all that is implied by the law of celibacy; I am fully determined to fulfil this obligation and to keep it totally, with God's assistance, to the very end.

Finally, I sincerely promise that, in accord with the sacred Canons, I will comply most obediently with all that my Superiors require of me and with all that the Church's discipline demands; and that I am ready to give an example of virtue both in deed and in word, so that my undertaking of so great an office may indeed be worthy of reward from God.

This I promise; this I vow; this I swear; may God assist me, and these His Holy Gospels, which I touch with my hand.

We ought not, therefore, to be surprised that our insecure and anxiety ridden Church leadership orders that these documents along with a detailed record of the candidate's seminary career be preserved so that, the seminary rector informed us, they can be used in evidence against him if at a later date he should seek laicization. An institution which so plainly mistrusts its full-time servants that it seeks to bind their loyalty by chains of oaths inevitably attracts few of its members to seek to enter such service.

Another way, rooted not in oaths and law but in loving service freely given, needs to be found.

5

The History of the Law of Clerical Celibacy

Have we not every right . . . to be accompanied by a Christian wife?

(1 Corinthians 9:4–5)

The most obvious sign of the absence of authentic freedom in proceeding to priestly ordination in the Roman Catholic Church is the imposition of compulsory celibacy on all candidates. The history of this regulation is not, we think, well known. In our experience, most Catholics assume that it has always been a feature of the Roman Catholic priesthood, that its justification exists in the Gospels and that it has always been freely and joyfully embraced by the overwhelming majority of priests. This is simply not true.

It *is* true, however, that those in charge of institutional religion seem to have a natural preferential option for celibacy – for its priests. Michael Pfliegler (in *Celibacy*, Sheed and Ward, 1967) notes that Cato (234–149 BC) ruled that 'No woman should be allowed to be present at holy rites, nor should she see how they are performed'. Sex, throughout history, has been perceived as a threat to priestly sanctity: for example, Indian Brahmins had a duty to their caste to produce one son, after which they withdrew into a life of solitude and penance; the Buddha is quoted as saying that 'the man who clings to wife and child stands in the tiger's jaws; there is no salvation for him'; in pre-Christian ancient Egypt, the 'Inclusi' of the temples at Memphis and Alexandria, together with 42 other temples all dedicated to Serapis (a kind of composite Greek-Egyptian god), were celibates; in Syria and Babylon, the priests of Astarte had to be celibate; priests and priestesses of Zeus in Greece were celibate, as were many philosophers; Hippocrates, the ancient physician whose name is recalled in the so-called hippocratic oath of doctors, is representative of the philosophers' attitude in his description of the sex act as 'a kind of mild epilepsy'; the Aztec priests of South America had a most severe celibacy discipline: any priests having contact with females were 'to be whipped to death'. Whenever they met a woman they had to lower their eyes to the ground. The Chief Priest was not even allowed to leave the temple, or to come in contact with women in any way, not even socially. If he violated these laws, his body was torn to pieces and his limbs given to his successor as a warning example.

Uta Ranke-Heinemann, the German professor of religious history at Essen University and the first woman ever to hold a chair of Catholic theology, tells us in her encyclopaedic *Eunuchs for Heaven* that cultic castration was common throughout the pagan Middle East. Three hundred years before Christ, Demosthenes was urging the necessity to 'practise continence for a certain number of days' before temple worship. Seventeen years before Christ, Tibullus forbade approach to the altar by 'all who have enjoyed the pleasures of love the previous night'. One hundred and twenty years after Christ, Plutarch was demanding at least one night's sleep after sex before sacrifice could begin.

Indeed, among ancient peoples, it seems that only the Jews neither had a celibate priesthood nor cultivated virginity as a religious virtue. Old Testament texts in favour of this particular form of asceticism are extremely difficult to find, whereas examples abound of citations of polygamy and multitudes of children as signs of the divine favour. But even the Old Testament seems to require abstinence from sexual relations at times of religious celebration. Behind this desire to separate sex from priesthood, or at least from worship, lies a conception of priesthood as sacred, set apart, cultic and devoted to worship.

Naturally enough, the first Christians, who were all convert Jews, followed Old Testament practice in not imposing the state of celibacy upon office holders in the Church. Neither does the New Testament lend any support to the view that sexual activity disqualifies any Christian from offering worship.

At the beginning of the Church, then, there was no law of celibacy. There was, of course, the saying of the Lord about those 'eunuchs who have made themselves so for the sake of the kingdom of heaven' (Matthew 19:12). St Paul had also praised celibacy on the grounds that it left a man or woman free to attend to the Lord's affairs (1 Corinthians 7:32–34), but neither of these amounted to a law. Jesus had said, 'Let anyone accept this who can' and Paul acknowledged that he was 'saying this only to help you, not to put a bridle on you'. In fact, as we know, some of the apostles were married, including Peter himself. St Paul asks rhetorically, 'Have we not every right . . . to be accompanied by a Christian wife, like the other apostles?'

(1 Corinthians 9:5). The author of the Epistle to Timothy expects a presiding elder or overseer (a word sometimes mistranslated 'bishop' – at that time, there were no bishops) to be married and to run an orderly personal household; he must be 'a man who manages his own household well and brings his children up to obey him and be well-behaved' (1 Timothy 3:4).

The first official Church legislation imposing celibacy was passed at the Spanish Synod of Elvira early in the fourth century. Recognizing the fact of clerical marriages, its canon 33 ruled that 'Bishops, priests and deacons, and all clergy in general who have altar service to perform, must refrain from intercourse with their wives, and are not allowed to beget children. If they oppose this, they forfeit their official position.' Although this was only a local synod, its rulings in fact were widely adopted by ecclesiastical authority throughout the West. Elvira's policy was undoubtedly prompted partly by the sharp rise in the number wishing to become priests. Since this increase in 'vocations' accompanied a decrease in persecution, the authorities not unreasonably feared the development of a laxer, less dedicated spirit among the clergy. Compulsory celibacy was seen as either a bracing influence or an efficient form of screening out unsuitable candidates. Furthermore, the notion was gaining ground that sexual activity and holiness were an ill-matched pair. To avoid sex, the argument ran, you must avoid marriage; but the clergy should avoid sex, therefore the clergy must avoid marriage.

Although the Council of Nicaea (325) resisted an attempt to extend the decrees of the Synod of Elvira to the whole Church, it nevertheless tightened discipline from New Testament times by making a positive law of the post-New Testament tradition that anyone who was single when he was ordained to the priesthood could not thereafter be allowed to marry. Moreover, some subsequent legislation clearly showed that it was sex rather than the legal fact of marriage which troubled the minds of some authorities. In 446, Pope Leo I declared in a letter to Bishop Rusticus of Narbonne, with apparent generosity: 'There is no need for them [priests] to leave their wives. They should consider themselves free from marriage, so that while marital love may remain yet the business of the wedding feast may cease.' In other words, priests could remain married technically, but they were not to make love to their wives (Pfliegler, *Celibacy*, p. 29). Ranke-Heinemann cites various instances of synodal legislation to the same effect: Arles (443), Orléans III (538), Clermont (535) and Orléans IV (541). It is worth recalling that by this time the Augustinian teaching on the inseparability of sin from marital sexual relations was well in place. St Augustine of Hippo, a major influence on Catholic moral teaching for centuries, taught that it was impossible for even married couples to have intercourse without at least venial sin. It is therefore little wonder that Pope Gregory I (Gregory the Great) informed Bishop Leo of Catania that a man married *before* ordination should 'love his wife like a sister and shun her like an enemy' *after* ordination.

In the ensuing centuries, the efforts to turn an essentially *legal* obligation into a personal vow were steadily intensified. Even deacons who were married were supposed to give up living sexually with their wives. This campaign by no means found an enthusiastic welcome among the clergy themselves. The regulations met with stubborn resistance. As late as the ninth century, a married man, Hadrian II, was elected pope. (See J. Blenkinsopp, *Celibacy, Ministry, Church*, Burns and Oates, 1969, p. 21.) As we shall see, throughout the centuries between Leo I's decree and the second Lateran Council (which sought to settle the matter once and for all), the authorities were forced constantly to repeat the legislation because so many priests, often with the support of their bishops, continued to exercise their inalienable human right to marry.

Draconian measures were used to enforce the law. The Synod of Tours (567), for instance, ordered surveillance of the clergy: 'The archpriest is always to have with him a cleric who accompanies him everywhere and must have his bed in the same room with him' to prevent his having intercourse with his wife. Canon 19 of that Synod even established a rota for this curious duty: 'Seven subdeacons, lectors or laymen can take it in turn to do this' (Ranke-Heinemann, p. 87). The provincial Council of Seville (592) labelled the sons of those in major orders as bastards, a declaration repeated 500 years later at the Synod of Bruges in 1031. Thirteen years earlier, the Synod of Pavia had invaded parental rights and outraged Christian consciences by declaring that children of priests were to be slaves of the Church. In 1049, Pope 'Saint' Leo IX included priests' wives in the same category. Pope Gregory VII (1073–85), in a letter to Bishop Bernold of Constance, described priestly marriage as the crime of fornication; what the apostle Paul, albeit reluctantly, had allowed as a safeguard against fornication became for the mediaeval pope the very sin which Paul had sought to guard against. By the twelfth century, at the first Lateran Council in 1123, the Church authorities sought to outlaw married clergy by declaring that any attempted marriages by those in major orders, that is, subdeacons, deacons or priests, were null and void. Pope Innocent II, at the Synod of Clermont in 1130, declared that the dignity of priests, as 'vessels of the Lord and sanctuaries of the Holy Ghost', was lowered if they 'lie in marriage beds and live in uncleanliness'. Finally, in 1139, and in the face of continued intense opposition from both priests and many bishops, the second Lateran Council decreed that marriage and the priesthood were mutually exclusive.

The Council's hopes of a final settlement were not fulfilled. In thirteenth-century Germany, many priests were openly and with episcopal permission celebrating their marriages. In Spain, the Synods of Valladolid (1322) and Valencia (1388) were still trying to enforce the law in the next century. A hundred years later, similar decrees had to be made all over again in Germany (at the Synod of Cologne, 1415) and France (Synod of Paris, 1429). (See Uta Ranke-Heinemann, pp. 94–8 for a much longer catalogue.) No doubt, poor communications were one reason for the widespread non-observance of the law which this repetition implies, but there is equally no doubt, from the angry reaction of the contemporary clergy, that the main reason was a different view of the inherent obligations of the priesthood. The Church authorities themselves, even at the time of the Council of Trent, recognized this fact in their original willingness to consider permitting the marriage of priests (along with the giving of the chalice to the laity!); the reformers, by making the abolition of celibacy a touchstone for Church reform, effectively blocked the offer of such a compromise from the Council fathers.

Since the Council of Trent, and with the implementation of the seminary method of training priests which effectively shuts them off from the world they are meant to serve, the law of celibacy has become thoroughly entrenched. But it is an entrenchment enforced against the will of the clergy themselves. The history of this law stands in sharp contradiction to Pope John Paul II's assertion in *Pastores Dabo Vobis* of the 'centuries-old choice which the Western Church has made and maintained – despite all the difficulties and objections raised down the centuries – of conferring the order of presbyter only on men who have given proof that they have been called by God to the gift of celibacy in absolute and perpetual chastity'.

The cast of mind behind this legislation is evident. A Church which regarded sin as almost inevitable in marriage could hardly allow its clergy to participate in such activities, particularly once those clergy began to be regarded as sacred persons. It was only in the early twentieth century, with Pope Pius X's advocacy of frequent, even daily Communion, that the taboo on receiving Communion the morning after sexual intercourse was finally swept away – at least officially. Some people to this day remain prejudiced against too close a link between sexual intercourse and Holy Communion. If in earlier centuries sexual intercourse was a bar to lay people receiving Communion, how much greater a bar it was to celebrating Mass.

Another major reason for this hardening attitude, already evident at Elvira, was the growth of monasticism. When the age of the great persecutions had passed, the life of the celibate monk was increasingly seen as the ideal for the Christian; his vows of obedience, poverty and chastity were the identification marks of this life. It would not have been suitable for the secular clergy to be outdone by their monastic brethren in what were considered to be the ideals of Christian holiness.

We must also accept the painful truth that the attitude of the official Church towards women was – and, sadly, in some instances still is – less than Christian. For Tertullian, a major teacher from the second to the third centuries, women are 'the Devil's Gateway [who] destroyed so easily God's image, man'. His contemporary, Origen, announced that God sees only the masculine and 'does not stoop to look upon what is feminine and of the flesh'. At the Synod of Elvira, the senior clergy revealed their contempt for women, forbidding them, for example, by canon 35, 'to spend the night in a cemetery since often under the pretext of prayer they secretly commit evil deeds', and by canon 67 'to have anything to do with long-haired men or hair-dressers'. Canon 81 decreed that 'Women shall not pre-sume on their own, without their husbands' signatures, to write to lay women who are baptized, nor shall they accept anyone's letters of peace addressed only to themselves' (see Walsh, McEwan and Brewster, *Celibacy in Control*, Kathleen Fedouloff). Augustine felt that 'nothing so casts down the manly mind from its height than the fondling of a woman'. Writing in the same fourth/fifth centuries, the famous preacher, St John Chrysostom, whose name means 'the golden-tongued', thought that a woman's 'bodily beauty is a white-washed tomb, for inside it is full of filth'. In those same centuries, Church law suggested that women should stay away from Communion when menstruating. In 460, the Synod of Tours repeated earlier prohibitions on intercourse between a priest and his wife on the grounds that priests were daily engaged in sacred mysteries. It is against this anti-sex, pro-ascetic, misogynist background that we have to judge the much stressed value of the Church tradition of clerical celibacy. History must place a question mark beside Pope Paul VI's description of celibacy as a centuries-old 'brilliant jewel' (*Sacerdotalis Caelibatus*, 1967, CTS translation).

The claim is often made that all this belongs to the past: however dubious the origins of the law of celibacy may have been, the defence runs, the grounds for its continuance are now far different. It is certainly true that positive arguments are advanced nowadays in favour of celibacy. Such arguments are perfectly reconcilable with the goodness of marriage and sex and imply no disrespect to women, and we shall be looking at some of these later. But there is a great deal of evidence which suggests that, fundamentally, the mentality of the Church authorities has not changed.

In his 1936 encyclical on the priesthood, Pope Pius XI argued that 'Since God is spirit, it seems proper that everyone who devotes and consecrates himself to his service should also, in a certain manner, free himself from his body'. The implication is that the married are less pure through enslavement to the body. Pope Pius XII's 1954 encyclical on sacred virginity repeats the eleventh-century St Peter Damien's demand that the daily celebration of Mass be accompanied by *perfect* chastity. Is married people's chastity imperfect, and is it edifying that a modern pope should quote with approval an eleventh-century saint who had described priests' wives as 'appetizing flesh of the devil', 'the cause of our ruin', 'harlots, prostitutes', 'wallowing places for fat pigs . . . parading the ardour of your ungovernable lust'? (See Walsh, McEwan & Brewster, op. cit., pp. 35–6.)

The History of the Law of Clerical Celibacy

Paul VI's 1967 encyclical on celibacy speaks of the priest's need to observe 'perfect chastity' no less than sixteen times. The clear implication is that everyone else's chastity is somehow imperfect. It is basic Christian morality that all human beings are bound to the full observance of chastity, that is, the proper management of their sexuality, the married no less than the celibate. The married simply accomplish it in different ways, but one is not a more perfect chastity than the other, as had been claimed by an earlier Catholic tradition of the inherent sinfulness of sex. Other sections of the encyclical practically deny to married people the possibility of a close relationship to Christ or of a total dedication to his Kingdom. Celibacy, we are told, is based on 'the choice of a closer and more complete relationship with the mystery of Christ' enabling priests to live 'a life wholly dedicated to . . . God's kingdom' (CTS edition, pp. 24–5). This hardly accords with Christ's call to *everyone* to holiness. The encyclical blinks, too, at history in its assertion that the reasons advanced for celibacy 'were always inspired by specifically Christian considerations' (p. 11) and that there was a 'spread through the East and West of the voluntary practice of celibacy by sacred ministers' (p. 18). As we have seen, it was imposed by law against opposition for centuries. It also pays less respect than is due to both the creation of human nature as human and to the Incarnation itself in its assertion that the ordained priest's sharing in the mission of Christ 'will be more perfect the freer the sacred minister is from the bond of flesh and blood' (Ibid., p. 12). In January 1970 the Dutch Bishops voted overwhelmingly for the abolition of priestly celibacy. Pope Paul VI's letter in response to their request for a reconsideration of the law was published in *L'Osservatore Romano*, and reprinted in full in *The Tablet* (14 February 1970).

Pope John Paul II will not even permit discussion of the issue but the current Roman attitude towards clerical celibacy is perhaps most vividly indicated both in the 1990 priesthood synod and in two recent Vatican decisions.

The first was the withdrawal of permission in 1989 to Mr David McDonald, a former Anglican priest, to be ordained virtually on the eve of his ordination solely because of the 'discovery' that he had married after becoming a Catholic. His ordination, the Papal Nuncio in England said, would have been to reverse the Church's tradition. To ordain married men who married before becoming Catholics does not, apparently, reverse this tradition.

The second concerned two Brazilian priests. These were married men, one of whom had been ordained as a deacon. In October 1990 – ironically while the Bishops were meeting with the Pope during the Synod called to discuss the priesthood – the Vatican announced that these two married men had been given special permission to be ordained as priests. A condition was attached to their ordination: they had to live with their wives as brothers and sisters. Cardinal Christian Wiyghan Tumi of Cameroon, one of the three papally appointed presidents of the synod, in the course of a press interview at which the matter was raised, blandly and apparently unperturbed stated that the marriage bond of these two men had not been broken but had simply been suspended. The Pope, he said, had given them 'permission to suspend the exercise of their marital rights'. Their wives and children had given their approval. (See *The Tablet*, 27 October 1990, p. 1386.) This scandalous decision, coupled with the strenuous efforts being made to deprive of their right to continue to function as priests those Czech married men, who were ordained as priests during World War II and who gave devoted service to their people, for no other reason than that they are married, amply demonstrates that Rome has not in essentials departed from its centuries old hostility to marriage, to women and to sexual love. Pope John Paul II's *Pastores Dabo Vobis* does nothing to mitigate this essentially negative attitude to sex and marriage. Celibacy, he says, must be considered 'as a value that is profoundly connected with ordination . . . as a man's choice of a *greater and undivided love for Christ and his Church*' (my italics). The message to the world is clear: marriage is an obstacle to the love of God and sex a notable impediment to a deep relationship with him, a depressing message reiterated as recently as July 1995 in the English bishops' pastoral letter, which declares that the priest's celibacy 'speaks eloquently of his total dedication to the Lord'.

6

Imposing a Law of Celibacy: the Consequences

About people remaining virgin,
I have no command from the Lord.
(1 Corinthians 7:25)

Despite the unhappy history of the law of clerical celibacy, both in its origins and in its development, many would argue that *in itself* it is a solid advantage for the Church, claiming scriptural support for their view. St Matthew's Gospel does indeed show Jesus praising those 'eunuchs who have made themselves so for the sake of the kingdom of Heaven' (19:12). But to claim that this text justifies compulsory celibacy demeans the language of scripture and ignores the total context. The use of the word 'eunuch' is significant: it denotes someone who has been castrated, who is actually incapable of sexual activity. Jesus could hardly have been literally advocating such a course, although the eminent early Church writer, Origen, thought he was. This is an instance, common enough in the New Testament, of Jesus using vivid and forceful language to express a particularly important point – that it is possible for some of his followers to be so absorbed by the Kingdom of God and the will to serve it totally that, *for them*, marriage is simply impossible. The Dutch Dominican theologian, Schillebeeckx, speaks of an 'existential inability to do otherwise'. (Cf *Clerical Celibacy Under Fire*, Sheed & Ward, 1968.) More important still, the context shows that Jesus explicitly sought to avoid giving his words the force of law. 'It is not everyone who can accept what I have said, but only to those to whom it is granted . . . Let anyone accept this who can' (Matthew 19:11–12).

St Paul also expounds the spiritual advantages of celibacy (1 Corinthians 7:32–39). His thesis is indisputable: those who have freely embraced a celibate life in order to devote themselves totally and directly to the service of the Kingdom undoubtedly will find a greater freedom in their lives; the Church has always needed and always will need such persons. There, indeed, is the real value of celibacy for the Church. Those who by their own untrammelled choice are entirely free, inwardly and outwardly, of personal, family and domestic ties, clearly offer a maximum availability for service. Great human endeavours in every field, not simply the religious, have always benefited from those who devote their lives entirely to an enterprise and there can be no enterprise greater than the spread of the Gospel.

But celibacy by itself will not achieve these benefits. The gift of celibacy is for others, not for the recipient of the gift. It must make him or her more, not less, loving; more, not less, human; kinder and gentler, not harsher and harder; more capable, not less, of forming loving relationships. Celibacy is meaningless if the void which it must inevitably leave in the person's human heart is filled with riches or ambition, fruitless activity or dubious pleasures. The end of all our being is God and our neighbour –

celibacy can be justified if it helps to make possible the attainment of that end. On any other ground, it has no meaning for the Kingdom.

Can, therefore, a *law* of celibacy promote or even safeguard these values? We have already seen that the New Testament not only knows no such law but explicitly excludes it. Jesus describes celibacy as a gift offered to some; Paul stresses that he is not attempting to impose an obligation. We surely are right at the very least to query the imposition as a component of ministry, which *is* necessary to the Church, an obligation which is *not* seen as necessary in the Church's foundation documents.

The previous chapter showed that the origins of this law lay, and its continuance still lies, in an extremely dubious understanding of both human sexuality and of women. It is also a fact that the demand for celibacy grew with the increasing identification of Christian ministry with the cultic, worship-centred priesthood of the Jews and of the pagans which was also suspicious of sexuality and of women. This is an attitude which has by no means been abandoned in the Church of today. We have noted Pope Paul VI's stress on the priest's need of perfect chastity and continence. Pope John Paul II used similar language in his 1979 Maundy Thursday letter to priests, and repeated it in *Pastores Dabo Vobis*. There is the possibility that the continuance of a law of celibacy is also a continuance of unchristian attitudes to humanity in general and to married people in particular, as well as to human sexuality and, indeed, to Christian revelation itself.

The imposition of this law on the grounds that it provides the supreme expression of total dedication to God's service is surely extremely offensive to clergy who are married. Such clergy exist, of course, within the Roman Catholic Church – increasingly so as more 'convert' married Anglican priests are admitted to Roman Catholic orders – and in non-Catholic churches, now recognized since Vatican II as part of the Church of Christ. The climate resulting from ecumenism has enabled Catholics, especially priests, to meet at much closer quarters the clergy of other churches, clergy who are married and who are yet no less wholehearted than themselves in their Christian service. It would be a very large claim indeed to maintain that the celibate Catholic priesthood exhibits *in its day-to-day reality*, whatever claims are made for it in theory, a greater dedication to God and to people than the married clergy in either our own or other Churches.

A very serious consequence of imposed celibacy for the Church as a whole is that it leaves government and direction in the Church entirely in the hands of a male élite. Church authority is becoming increasingly sensitive in this area. In his Maundy Thursday 1995 address to priests, defending the refusal to ordain women, Pope John Paul II makes the remarkable assertion, 'Certainly the question [of not ordaining women] could be put in these [discriminatory] terms if the hierarchical priesthood granted a social position of privilege characterized by the exercise of "power". But this is not the case: the ministerial priesthood, in Christ's plan, is an expression not of domination but of service.' This extraordinary statement will not, I think, bear the scrutiny by history of the development of hierarchical power in exclusively male hands. The plain fact is that the direct insights of married men and of all women have been denied their proper influence on the shaping of Church teaching, discipline and policy. Only very recently has there been any sign at all of a willingness to listen to the experience of more than half the Church's membership, and even that willingness is very limited. When Archbishop Quinn, the representative of the American bishops, and our own Cardinal Hume, during the 1980 Synod on the family, tried to have considered the actual experience of married people which contradicted the assertions of papal authority on the nature of family life and of couples' sexual experience, they were simply ignored. (See P. Hebblethwaite, *Introducing John Paul II*, Fount Paperbacks, 1982, pp. 135–140.) Detailed teaching on matters where the teachers lack direct knowledge – where, quite literally (and I do not mean this disrespectfully), they do not *know* what they are talking about – is bound to raise doubts about its validity in the minds of those taught.

The consequences for the Church are not good: on the one hand, we are very likely to have a fundamentally distorted presentation of the meaning of Christian commitment in our ever more complex world; on the other, a growing indifference to every statement which emanates from an authority which refuses to look beyond its own ranks for enlightenment in its teaching.

Nonetheless, the claim continues to be made that appreciation within the Church of the gift of celibacy will be lost without the safeguard of a law of celibacy. We need to be quite clear that we *are* here dealing with law. The significance of that last point needs to be stressed. Church authority increasingly presents what is certainly a law as a vow. The essence of a vow is that it is a freely undertaken promise to God. But secular priests, that is, most priests who work in a parish, do not in a real sense take a vow of celibacy, unless of course they do so privately. Their commitment to celibacy arises from their acceptance of the Church's law. When a candidate approaches ordination, to both diaconate and priesthood, he is compelled to accept celibacy if he wishes to be ordained. To describe this procedure as a freely undertaken vow is to distort language. The man is seeking, ultimately, the priesthood; he knows that he cannot be a priest unless he also accepts celibacy. The focus of the decision is, therefore, not on the value of celibacy as such, but on the priesthood itself. Celibacy is part of the price he pays for that. Students for the priesthood are not genuinely free to consider celibacy as a personally chosen option. The obligation of celibacy, like the course of studies and the whole order of seminary life, has to be seen as part and parcel of the total price which has to be paid for what is regarded as the inestimable privilege of being a priest. It is doubtful if whatever is said about celibacy as an expression of total dedication to God and one's fellow human beings plays *in reality* a very great part in the students' *conscious* acceptance of celibacy. They want above all to be priests; to be a priest, they have to be celibate – it is as simple, as deceptively simple, as that. In other words, the very existence of a law of celibacy attached to the priesthood, as distinct from a vow sought in its own right, poses the risk that those wishing sincerely to be priests will pay scant attention to the values supposed to be attached to the content of that law itself.

The Church leadership's policy on the training of priests by its very nature involves the suppression of freedom. In his encyclical on the priesthood, Pope Paul VI emphasizes that 'care should be taken for the progressive development of his [the candidate's] personality through the means of physical, intellectual and moral education directed towards the control and personal dominion of his instincts, sentiments and passions' (§65). He must accept 'the personal and community type of discipline demanded by the priestly life. Such a régime ... should not be borne only as an imposition from without. It should be inculcated and implanted within the context of the spiritual life as an indispensable component' (§66). Rather contradictorily, some may feel, the Pope continues: 'The complete education of the candidate to the priesthood ought to be directed to help him acquire a tranquil, convinced and free choice of the grave responsibilities which he must assume in conscience before God and the Church' (§69). The difficulty is that, effectively, the choice has already been made about celibacy from the moment he comes to the seminary. The tell-tale phrase is 'guided liberty': the candidate, says the Pope, will practise humility and obedience as expressions of internal truth and of 'a guided liberty' which will produce 'a balanced personality, strong and mature, a combination of inherited and acquired qualities, harmony of all his powers in the light of the faith' (§70).

I have already described the procedures in force to try to bind both candidates for the priesthood and the ordained clergy by solemn oaths, procedures suggestive of a profound lack of trust. These latest requirements are a further stage in a well established policy of mistrust and coercion. In February 1970, hard on the heels of calls in the Church, especially in Holland, for an end to obligatory celibacy, the Roman Congregation for the Clergy issued an instruction to Catholic priests throughout the world annually to renew their promises of celibacy and obedience. The priest press officer of the Congregation, in presenting the instruction to the media, expressly located it in the context of those priests who 'question certain truths of the faith and some of the foundations of Christian and priestly life, and tend towards a radical secularization'. The same instruction warned that for the task of training future priests 'Only priests who think with the Church and do not let themselves go astray from its tenets should be chosen' (*The Tablet*, 14 February 1970, p. 163).

The unpalatable fact is that the law of celibacy operates within a wider, oppressive structure. In *Pastores Dabo Vobis*, Pope John Paul II writes of the need to maintain 'a scrupulous respect for the nature of theology', adding that 'true theology proceeds from faith and aims at leading to the faith', propositions which of course no believing Christian would dispute. But it soon becomes evident that 'faith' is being given a very particular meaning here which in practice identifies it with the views of the teaching authority. 'The whole of theology,' he says, 'is ordered to nourishing the faith', and 'Faith is the point of departure and the point of arrival of theology.' Here, the Pope appears to be presenting 'the faith' as though it were a given entity existing before and altogether apart from theology, whereas from the moment that we begin to make a response to the proclamation of the Gospel (in itself a theological act), we are 'doing' theology, albeit in a rudimentary form. The 'official teaching of the Church', a concept very dear to Pope John Paul II, is of course a highly sophisticated form of theology. It is consequently difficult both to assent to and not to be alarmed by the thinking lying behind the Pope's assertion of the need to distinguish 'the common teaching of the Church from the opinions of theologians'. The papal view fails to allow sufficient weight to the truth that 'the common teaching of the Church' is itself the outcome of theological reflection, doubtless under the guidance of the Holy Spirit. If we grant to theologians who are selected (and they *are* selected) to advise the Roman magisterium a degree of divine inspiration denied to be possessed by other theologians equally qualified and doubtless equally holy, we are surely in danger of turning the already grave menace of 'creeping infallibility' into a Gadarene rout which would take all teaching and all theology over the cliffs of credibility. Especially in a community claiming to be inspired by the Holy Spirit there is no need for a stranglehold on intellectual freedom.

This line of approach is singularly ill-suited to the nature of Christ's Church and can hardly be good for the priest's own development, maturity and psychic balance. There is some scientific evidence that it is not. In his book, *Whatever Happened to Vatican II?*, Michael Winter quotes a survey carried out in the early 1970s on priests in the United States and Europe which 'concluded that 10 to 15 per cent are psychologically mature, 60 to 70 per cent are emotionally immature, and 20 to 25 per cent present serious psychiatric difficulties'. Another piece of research on a group of 271 American priests found that '7 per cent were "developed", 18 per cent were developing, 66.5 per cent were under-developed and 8.5 per cent were maldeveloped' (p. 166). Even allowing for the deficiencies of such investigations, the picture is still alarming.

One of the chief, and certainly most attractive, arguments for celibacy is that it enables the priest to be fully available to his people. Unencumbered by the cares of wife, family and home, he can give himself entirely to his pastoral mission. Freedom from marriage leaves him freedom for the work of the Kingdom. Where celibacy is embraced in full freedom and with the fervent desire to use to the full the availability which it makes possible, then the benefits to the Church and to the priest himself are incalculable. But we have to ask ourselves if all these conditions are always fulfilled in practice. If an enforced celibacy actually has a crippling effect upon the priest's own character and personality; if he is not truly called to the life of loneliness which it entails; if observance of the law diminishes his capacity to love, then the priest actually becomes, whatever the theory, *less* available to his people, not more. Whereas, the experience of loving and being loved within the unique relationship of marriage can so expand a person's character and psychic resources as to vastly increase his or her openness to others. After all, it is possible to argue that by learning the meaning of love within marriage, a priest might then become a more loving person and thereby be better equipped to serve his people in the fullest possible charity. There is – at the very least, surely – room for both celibate and married servants of the People of God.

We also need to think about the effect of compulsory celibacy on the actual situation of some individual priests. If we are to be a truly Christian People of God, we cannot shut our eyes to the suffering of so many of our priests. This is not a problem which is very often aired publicly, for reasons which are only too obvious. There are many truly dedicated and devoted priests who find the law of celibacy an obstacle to their ministry, a block to their human development, a distortion of their manhood and a barrier to their ability to relate to others, either men or women. Many enter into situations which fill them with guilt and which impose great suffering on themselves and their partners, but in which they nevertheless feel they are following a law higher than man's. Clare Jenkins' recent book, *A Passion for Priests* (Hodder Headline, 1995), provides a compassionate insight into the anguish – for priest and partner alike – which exists. She insists that the accounts she provides 'are not isolated cases. Every one of these women knows someone else in a similar situation. For every sensational case that hits the headlines, for every Annie Murphy and Bishop Eamonn Casey, there are scores that remain hidden because the women lack the desire, the courage or the anger to speak out' (pp. 8–9). We are baffled that Church authority is able to view with apparent equanimity the injustice done here to innumerable women and men by its refusal openly to investigate this horrendous situation.

There is, indeed, ever increasing evidence that, for all the claims made for celibacy, it is not in fact widely observed among those supposedly vowed to it. Dr A. W. Richard Sipe, a former priest and now a practising clinical psychologist, from his 25-year study of celibacy among Roman Catholic priests, *A Secret World: sexuality and the search for celibacy*, concludes that nearly half the Roman Catholic priests in the United States either temporarily or permanently do not observe strict celibacy. (See *The Tablet*, 19 January 1991, pp. 69–70.) Dr Jack Dominian, the highly respected English Catholic psychiatrist, in reviewing the book in *The Tablet*, expresses reservations about its conclusions. But he stresses that 'the survey was carried out with care, and cannot easily be dismissed or ignored'. Dr Dominian offers little comfort to those who would say that the American experience cannot be extended to this country. He writes: 'I can only say that in my professional capacity I myself have met virtually all the problems to which Sipe refers' and he clearly has little doubt that a proper survey would confirm that our situation is essentially no different. Clare Jenkins has interviewed women from around the world: Germany, South Africa, France, USA, Holland, Belgium, Austria, Switzerland, Italy, Spain and Ireland. The evidence is that throughout these countries there are hundreds, if not thousands, of actively sexual relationships between priests and women. She quotes the belief of one woman active within the higher echelons of the Church that 'there is a general and non-judgemental acceptance that more priests are in relationships than are not'. Clare Jenkins adds that this statement was subsequently confirmed by a senior Jesuit (p. 8).

There is also an increasingly difficult situation arising from the tragically growing frequency of child abuse cases. Many have rightly pointed out that child abusers, whether priestly or lay, are not restricted to the ranks of the celibate. At the same time, it is difficult not to think that the law of celibacy aggravates the problems of these offenders. I have no doubt that the compulsory celibacy rule has an enormous amount to do with the cases of sexual abuse by priests which are coming to light. This is not to say that these men would not have offended if only they had been allowed to marry. The problem is probably much more to do with the sexual climate in the Church which is responsible for the law of celibacy. No matter how much the Vatican denies it, and no matter how often the Pope talks about availability and dedication to one's people, the plain fact is that the underlying reason – and often *not* so underlying – is the belief that sexual activity is incompatible with real holiness. This is why so many Catholics associate, and are intended to associate, the priesthood with 'freedom' from the claims of sex.

This poses a particular danger for many men, especially those with a very 'high' doctrine of priestly dignity, who believe they have a vocation to the priesthood. They then have enormous difficulty in coming to terms with the fact that they still experience sexual feelings, desires, fantasies and so on. They believe that entering the imagined sexless state of the priesthood will deliver them from all these disturbances, and for a time, perhaps for a long time, they find this is true. But possibly because they have probably suppressed through the years 'normal' sexual urges, nature eventually asserts itself and does so perhaps in ways like paedophilia. This may well not begin evilly. With their natural desire for a heterosexual (or, of course, homosexual) relationship crushed, mangled and suppressed, it is easy to understand that many priests believe that their affection for children is innocent and good – and so it may well be, in the beginning. But because they have never come to terms with the fact that to be human is to be sexual, they do not understand the signs and the dangers, and tragedy results, perhaps especially in priests who are basically good, tender and loving. I know of no research to confirm scientifically any of this, but it seems to me to make sense. There are, of course, some men who become priests (or nurses, teachers, youth leaders, etc.) precisely because they are looking for a cover for what they know is base self-indulgence, but these I would imagine and certainly hope are in a minority.

The response of the Church authorities in the past was, and evidently in certain areas still is, both unreasonable and counterproductive. If they can evade the civil authorities, they do so, preferring to put these men into Catholic clerical institutions for 'treatment', which inevitably reinforces all the problems that gave rise to the situation in the first place. Catholic authority insists nowadays how important proper sexual education is in seminaries and how necessary it is that priests should have a healthy and balanced approach to sex. But since all such statements are flatly contradicted by the law of celibacy which rules out all possibility of free choice in the matter, there can be not only, in my view, no hope of an improvement but a much greater chance of even worse evils ensuing.

It is obvious that the present state of affairs cannot be good for the Church or for its mission to continue Christ's work in the world. It is true that efforts are being made to overcome the loneliness inseparable from a celibate life. These take the shape of encouraging priests to live in community where possible, though this is hardly an option open to most priests working in parishes. Moreover, a community life is not one which appeals to all priests: if they did not directly choose celibacy, even less did they directly choose to live with other priests – the religious life is a quite separate vocation. Another recent solution is what is known as the Ministry to Priests. This is a method of encouraging friendship, openness and mutual counselling among the clergy. To some extent it is a complete reversal of the ban on particular friendships, a ban which used to be so much a feature of seminary training. I have heard several priests speak approvingly of this development and certainly it has helped many of them. The fact remains that it is no substitute for marriage. That is a human relationship unique in human experience. There can indeed be excellent reasons for sacrificing it, but no one should be under the impression that anything else is an adequate substitute.

There is also a bitter irony in the argument that celibacy increases the priest's availability to his people. There can be no doubt that the law of celibacy is a major factor in the present shortage of priests. A 1984 report in the United States found that compulsory celibacy 'emerges constantly as a major negative factor' when vocations are investigated. Those seminarians who persevere in seeking ordination will tend to have certain psychological characteristics: 'recruitment . . . favoured the ordination of men who are "more dependent, institutionally orientated, sexually indifferent, and conservative"' (*The Tablet*, 23 June 1984, p. 599). Bishops from South America, Asia and Africa testify to the urgent need to ordain married men if they are to have sufficient priests. In these countries, and now more and more in the West too, there is an abundance of men and of women who are qualified to organize liturgical meetings, to preach, to distribute Holy Communion, to catechize – in fact, to do everything except pronounce the words of consecration and of absolution. The only barrier to their being able to consecrate and to absolve is that they are married or that they are women. For the sake of a man-made Church law, millions are denied the sacrament of Our Lord's body and blood. 'Except you eat my flesh and drink my blood,' said Jesus, 'you cannot have life in you.' The Church authorities have amended this text: 'Except you eat my flesh and drink my blood, provided at the hands of a male celibate priest, you cannot have life in you.'

In his closing address to the 1990 Synod of Bishops on the priesthood, Pope John Paul II categorically ruled out the slightest consideration of ordaining married men, let alone permitting celibacy to be optional. He regards such a suggestion merely as part of an attack on celibacy made with 'support and complicity in some of the mass media'. Such language from anyone other than this Pope would be regarded as showing scant respect for or trust in those who legitimately hold differing theological and pastoral positions. The Pope's own solution to the shortage of priests is to encourage 'dioceses more richly endowed with priests' to 'intensify' their help to 'those which are lacking' (*The Tablet*, 3 November 1990). This 'solution' presupposes that there are dioceses so 'richly endowed', that the transference of, say, Polish clergy to South America or the South Bank poses no cultural problems and that it would meet with the approval of the local hierarchy. It is certainly not a practical measure for areas of the Church where the priest to people ratio is 1 to 10,000, 20,000 and, in northeast Brazil, 45,000. The rigidity of the Pope's insistence upon celibacy is depriving hundreds of millions of the poorest among the People of God of what is meant to be the heart and centre of our faith. The celibacy law may not be the only cause of the shortage of priests; it is certainly a major one. The argument for celibacy of availability has, therefore, considerable weaknesses. Can the Vatican really justify before God its continued insistence upon a law which is raising such barriers to holiness among the People of God who are the Church?

This is not to criticize the notion of celibacy for the sake of the kingdom. It is a positive value and we know no one who seeks to abolish it. It is a gift to the Church. Many, many priests and lay people joyfully accept the sacrifices which it entails and are able to use it to deepen their love for God and for people. But it is surely right to question its value when it is presented by law as an obligation without which a man cannot serve the people of God as a priest. If, as the authorities constantly claim, priests do freely choose celibacy, there is simply no need of a law. But if they are not freely choosing it, no law can give it its proper value. All of us, priest or lay, married or single, man or woman, adult or child, are called to dedication and sacrifice. The command to love, to love God and to love our neighbour, is addressed equally to us all. Jesus did not envisage a two-tier holiness among his followers. Each of us must answer God's call, freely and lovingly, in his or her own way. For some, this will be by following the hard and lonely path of celibacy; for others, the self-sacrificing and selfless path of marriage. To all of us is given the opportunity to make our own the response of St Peter, our first – and married – Pope: 'Lord, you know everything; you know I love you' (John 21: 17).

7

The Sexual Dimension of Christian Life

The flash of love is a flash of fire,
a flame of Yahweh himself.
(Song of Songs 8:6b)

In *Shattered Vows*, David Rice cites an appalling but, sadly, not unique, example of clerical cynicism towards and ignorance of the place of sex in a loving relationship. A young priest admitted to his parish priest that he was having difficulties with the law of celibacy. His worldly-wise parish priest gave him some advice which he summed up in the aphorism, 'If you want a drink of milk, you don't have to buy the bloody cow'. My wife and I have found extraordinary difficulty in trying to bring some priests to an intelligent and sensitive understanding of what the sexual dimension of their relationship means to a happily married couple. From discussions with priests and from listening to public statements from the hierarchy, we have to conclude that far too many clerics still think of sex simply as a highly dangerous pleasure which marriage, under stringent conditions, legitimizes. This is, of course, hardly surprising. The law of celibacy prevents every priest from experiencing sex with any sense of freedom, exhilaration or joy. If he

83

observes the law, its nature is unknown to him: we recall the near wistfulness with which Cardinal Heenan once answered a journalist's question by saying that he had at times wondered what sexual intercourse was like. If, on the other hand, a priest does not observe the law, the ensuing guilt and subterfuge involved make impossible any proper appreciation of the authentic nature of committed sexual intercourse. This chapter has been written in the hope that we may be able to bring to the Church's celibate pastors a better understanding of the relationship between sex and love and so, perhaps, lessen a little those fears of the supposed dangerous consequences for the Church of removing the law of celibacy.

Presumably most Catholics, including our bishops, have a general idea of the history of mistrust of sex in the Church. I doubt that many are aware of the full extent and depth of that mistrust which certainly accounts for the present fear of sex. For centuries, the Church leadership and membership have regarded sex as a threat to the Christian life. Its only possible justification was the fact that it made possible the continuation of the human race. One of the principal sources of this stance was Stoic philosophy, which made procreation the sole justification of sexual activity. Highly influential Catholic writers like Clement of Alexandria and Origen enthusiastically adopted this standpoint and the barriers were raised against any consideration of sexual intercourse as an expression of love. Even more influential in a negative way were the first- and second-century AD groups called the Gnostics. They believed that they were a privileged élite who alone knew the full truth of the Gospel. They were opposed to marriage and to procreation and their ideas threatened to engulf much of early Christian teaching. Against them, the Church authorities rightly insisted constantly upon the goodness of marriage and the goodness of procreation. But the reaction to the powerful Stoic influence left no room for looking at sex save as the means of procreation. This emphasis inevitably led, for example by St Ambrose, the fourth-century bishop of Milan, to the condemnation of intercourse by the old or with the pregnant, even when they were married.

A further complication in the development of official teaching on sex was the freedom allowed by Roman law to parents in the disposal of their children. There was no penalty for parents who perpetrated infanticide, abandonment or abortion. Christians reacted against this by condemning all interference with life, or with what was considered to be the life-giving process and that included intercourse. What we would call 'contraception', at that time was called 'parricide' or 'the killing of a man-to-be'. As John T. Noonan says in his excellent book *Contraception*, 'The need to protect life, the need to defend procreation – these are the needs which guide the development of Christian thought on contraception' (New American Library, 1967, p. 119). Those same vital needs caused the Church authorities altogether to neglect the possibility of there being other dimensions than the procreative to marital sex.

Two further major influences on official Catholic teaching about sex arose towards the end of the third century: the heresy of the Manichees and the conversion of Augustine. The Manichees were understood to believe that marriage, intercourse and procreation were evil, following from their alleged belief that all these things served to perpetuate the kingdom of darkness. The Church leadership, of course, condemned their teaching. Unfortunately, in doing so it went to the opposite extreme, seeing the sole value of sex in its procreative purpose. Manicheeism had been condemned before Augustine became a Christian. As a former Manichee himself, and with the personal psychological problems arising from his own sexual experience, it was inevitable that his own condemnation of the group – with all the authority which that would convey – should be even more absolute. He taught that all sexual intercourse between the married which does not have as its sole purpose the procreation of children, is sinful, though not always mortally so – *that*, he said, depended on the degree of lust the couple brought to their activity.

This denial of the value and purpose of sex for any purpose outside the procreative became ingrained in Catholic theology. One major reason for this was the prestige of the monasteries, which had, in effect, preserved European civilization. The monks, themselves of course unmarried, based their condemnation of intercourse which sought to avoid conception largely on St Jerome's description of it as homicide and on its association with pagan magic practices – the term for magic, *maleficium*, was also a synonym for a sterilizing act. On this uncertain foundation, therefore, of Augustinian vehemence and monkish ignorance, the deeply rooted Catholic tradition that sex is solely for conception was built. Among the more striking instances of extreme teaching was Pope Gregory the Great's (590–604) *Pastoral Rule*, wherein the married were admonished that they might copulate only to produce children; they were also reminded that if any pleasure was mixed with the act of intercourse they had committed sin (Noonan, op. cit., p. 187).

This teaching was to be repeated several times down the ensuing centuries (see Noonan, pp. 240–242). The possibility of other developments was also prevented by the re-emergence of the ancient Gnostic and Manichee view that procreation and marriage are evils among a tenth-century group calling itself the Cathars (the Pure). Many of them, however, excluded from this condemnation non-procreative intercourse by the unmarried, which was indeed often celebrated in contemporary love poetry. Church authorities at the second Lateran Council of 1139 sought the assistance of the civil authorities in the suppression of these heretics, who by that stage were achieving considerable success in winning adherents to their views that sexual activity within marriage is mortally sinful and that procreation is evil because all flesh is evil. This doctrine did not prevent many Cathars from indulging in sexual licence, apparently on the grounds that such behaviour outside marriage was only an affair of the body, the real self not coming under any moral prohibitions. It is not difficult to understand the orthodox Catholic reaction: the only permissible intercourse was declared to be that between the married and for the purpose of procreation; the alternative sexual doctrine of the Cathars would not, and could not, be given a hearing.

But we must not lose sight of the fact that orthodox Catholicism also regarded sexual intercourse as sinful: it was simply that the intention to procreate (within marriage, of course) excused it – this was the central Augustinian principle, graphically expressed by Pope Innocent III, 'Who does not know that conjugal intercourse is never committed without itching of the flesh, and heat and foul concupiscence, whence the conceived seeds are befouled

87

and corrupted?' (*On the Seven Penitential Psalms*, 4, *Patrologia Latina*, p. 217, quoted in Noonan, op. cit., p. 242). Little wonder, then, that sexual activity was in general seen as incompatible with the Christian life. According to nature, the moral theologians said, sexual intercourse is permissible only between a man and wife, the man above the woman with insemination resulting. In addition, the couple have consciously to intend to produce a child. Any departure from this norm is to sin against the order of nature established by God. Our modern notion of intercourse as an expression of love was grimly classed as mortal sin. St Bridget, in her *Revelations*, warns husbands with pretty wives and wives with lovable husbands to be careful (Noonan, op. cit., pp. 299ff.).

From about the middle of the fifteenth century, we begin to see some weakening in this insistence that sexual intercourse can be justified only by the intention to procreate. A few writers began to countenance the idea only occasionally mooted earlier that sex was permissible to avoid fornication. And one, Martin Le Maistre, began to explore the idea that because sex was good as created by God it could not be sinful for married people to enjoy it (Ibid., p. 372). Le Maistre's theories were inevitably treated with great caution and indeed at first seem only to have been used to justify the use of sex to avoid fornication. Gradually, his ideas found wider acceptance so that even the Council of Trent in the sixteenth century was able to speak approvingly of love between husband and wife as a value in marriage, albeit in a very spiritual form. Nevertheless, by the end of the seventeenth century, teaching, largely under the influence of St Alphonsus Ligouri, had reached the stage of accepting the lawfulness of 'chaste touchings' between man and wife, with risk of ejaculation, provided there is 'urgent need for showing signs of affection to foster mutual love' (Ibid., p. 396). This somewhat crude language is a long way from a modern theology of marriage, but at least it gave hope of change. Sadly, despite advances in recent years, I am quite sure that this negative attitude towards sex persists. It seems difficult to persuade Catholics, lay as well as clerical, that sexual activity can be not only compatible with holiness but also be an integral part of it. Perhaps the difficulty lies in a misunderstanding of the nature of holiness.

We all know that holiness means closeness to God. But it is instructive to examine our images of holy people. They easily tend to be negative. Holy people are people who *don't* do certain things, like swearing, drinking, gambling or being frivolous. We certainly don't expect holy people to be very involved in worldly activities, although the popular image of holiness does not seem to find it incompatible with considerable wealth. And, of course, we particularly expect certain groups of Christians to be holy, like priests, monks and nuns, which leaves many feeling that the ordinary person living in the world, especially when such persons are married, can only be moderately holy. This idea is further reinforced by the fact that the overwhelming number of canonized saints – those officially declared to have been very holy indeed – do in fact belong to these groups.

The *essence* of holiness, however, does not consist at all of such activities; neither is it confined to nor even guaranteed by certain states of life. Certainly, it does involve closeness to God and such closeness is unlikely to be achieved without prayer and, normally, celebrating the sacraments. But we need to be on our guard against identifying the means with the end: prayer and the sacraments are *means* to holiness; participating in them does not *constitute* holiness.

It is interesting that the word 'holy' has exactly the same root as the word 'whole'. It indicates wholeness, integrity, balance. Holy people are people who are whole, sane and balanced in their lives; people who are true to themselves, to their natures. For believing Christians, this means being true to God's intentions for us, striving to be what he intends us to be, being dedicated to God's purposes for us precisely as human beings. Every human being, therefore, who dedicates himself or herself to God's purposes for them is holy, is a saint. That is why St Paul, writing to the Church in Rome, describes Christians – *all* Christians, that is – as 'saints': their baptism has consecrated them to God's purposes, although obviously such baptism is effective only if the baptized try to live out the consequences of such formal consecration.

The fact that we are all, without exception, called to holiness is a fundamental idea in the New Testament. Matthew 5:48 really sums up the whole of the Sermon on the Mount: 'You must therefore set no bounds to your love, just as your heavenly Father sets none to his.' This is a modern translation of the older, more familiar, but little heeded, 'You are to be perfect as your heavenly Father is perfect'. The important thing to notice here is that these words were addressed to *all* Christ's hearers; Jesus did not turn and speak to a group of Sisters of Mercy or members of the Cistercian contemplative order. He was speaking to people for whom the daily struggle to survive must have occupied all their attention: to people in religious and civil authority, to policemen and tax-gatherers, shepherds and fishermen, widows and teenagers, to the crippled and the mentally defective, to the unemployed and employers; in a word, to the motley crowd which make up humanity. It is on the basis of these words that the Second Vatican Council, a little stiffly perhaps, stated that 'all are called to sanctity and have received an equal privilege of faith through the justice of God' (*Lumen Gentium*, IV, 32, quoted in Abbott, ed., p. 58). Pope John Paul II has repeated this teaching in his document on the laity, *Christifideles Laici*, where he speaks of the primacy given to 'the call of every Christian to holiness'.

Holiness, then, means being true to God's purposes for us, that is, being true to ourselves as we are meant to be – being *whole* human beings. I do not think that I need to labour the point that we cannot be true to God's purposes for us unless we are people who love. The whole Bible, and especially the New Testament, again and again stresses that love is the foundation of a truly godly life. We are stultified as human beings unless we recognize that the first call upon us is to love God with our whole heart and – *at the same time* – our neighbour as ourselves. Love is of the very essence of our humanity.

This truth must affect our thinking about sexuality, especially sexuality within marriage. The sexual dimension to marriage is not an obstacle to holiness which the grace of marriage manages to overcome, but is, on the contrary, one of the most potent sources of holiness for the couple. It really ought to be easy to see how marriage, properly understood, fits into the notion of holiness. From the point of view of both the partners and of the second Vatican Council (*Gaudium et Spes*, S. 48, quoted in Abbott, ed., pp. 250ff.), marriage is ideally a *relationship*, a relationship of permanent, mutual, total self-giving, in which the partners are set aside for and consecrated for each other, a relationship in which they have a unique love for each other. This is precisely what holiness is. Holiness is about dedication, giving, service and love. Marriage is essentially about all those things and is therefore of itself, not because it has come to be regarded as a sacrament, holy. It is, in fact, the inbuilt goodness and holiness of marriage that make it a fit subject for sacramental status.

The next step follows logically. Since marriage is of its essence holy, all that the couple do which genuinely expresses their married relationship, is necessarily holy too. Time given to household affairs, to playing with the children, ferrying them to school or to their leisure pursuits, to the 101 items which make up the daily life of married people is not time which prevents people from being in touch with God. It is living the life that God asks of them. This is obviously not to say that married people do not need to pray or to celebrate the sacraments; they need that sort of 'direct' contact with God as much as anyone else. But we also need to be clear that those are not somehow the 'really' holy, much less the *sole* holy activities in our lives. We must never allow ourselves to feel that what goes to make up the very fabric of our married life is not in itself holy.

It is vital for the health of our thinking about sex to recognize that all this applies with particular force to sexual intercourse within marriage. We would appeal here directly to our priests and our bishops to heed the experience of couples who truly love each other and who have managed to free themselves of the negative notions which have undoubtedly coloured Catholic ideas about sex and marriage in relation to holiness.

For them, sexual intercourse is the expression, at the deepest level, of their love for each other; it is their most articulate expression of love, because it enables them to say, in a language which goes beyond all words, all – or almost all – that they feel for each other. Ideally, the sexual intercourse of the married can be described as the language in which the partners express in the deepest and fullest possible way their dedication to each other, their consecration of themselves to each other. We need to allow to sink into our hearts and minds the implications of the common and very attractive, despite its frequent misapplication, description of sexual intercourse as love-making. Ideally, that is *exactly* what we are talking about when we speak of sexual activity within marriage: making love, building up love between the partners, and then – because it is impossible truly to love another without at the same time becoming a more loving person oneself – extending the circle and influence of love in the world. In a very real sense, we can say that a married couple's love-making is the holiest thing they do; it is the finest expression of the holiness of their relationship and it opens them up towards those outside their own unique relationship, helping them to love others as they love themselves and finally, to love the God who made them and in whom all relationships find their ultimate consummation.

We need to stress this outward-looking aspect of married love. Our modern culture stresses the inward-looking nature of sexual love: songs, books and films all insist upon what the couple are *to each other*. This is, obviously, a vitally important aspect of marriage, but we cripple our understanding of the relationship if we think that it ends there. Where the intercourse of the married is truly making love, that is, the making of more and more love between the partners, it inevitably has the effect of making them more loving persons; they become more open to others because of the closeness effected between themselves. They see that no true love can remain centred on themselves; it must move their hearts and their minds to others – and this is, of course, of the very essence of holiness. When love-making is understood in this way, the couple are brought very close indeed to the heart of God, who, St John tells us, is Love itself.

Couples do not often expose publicly their innermost feelings about this most intimate aspect of their lives. But we are quite sure that many will confirm that the moments when they are closest to each other are the moments when they feel closest to God, and their sigh for each other is also a sigh for the God who has given them both this love and this means of expressing it. This is partly because sexual intercourse is an intensely humbling experience. We become aware of our littleness, of the gulf between what we want to say and to be and what we actually are; we become aware that we are worthwhile only because we are loved, loved first by this other human being and ultimately, by God whose voice and touch are to be discerned in these most sacred moments.

I speak, of course, of ideals. We are not suggesting that this is how it feels all the time or even most of the time. Our humanness too easily gets in the way. Yet I remain convinced that married Christians should never wholly lose sight of the ideal, should never allow them-selves to think that theirs is the lesser vocation, that they are offering God a second-best. Such a view is little short of insulting, not to say blasphemous, to God who has made us human and has bestowed upon us the gift of our sexuality. It surely makes no sense to suggest that automatically and in every case to deny to priests the fruits of this gift will thereby produce better priests.

I feel sure that one of the major obstacles to the Church's mission to bring the Good News of Christ to the world, and to the necessary rethinking of the law of celibacy for priests, is the failure to accept our sexuality with everything that it implies. Too often, both in the past and in the present, our view of holiness has been coloured by the notion that, to come near to God, we must go far from sex, and must overcome our lower nature, our baser instincts. I am firmly convinced that human beings do not have a lower nature and that none of our natural instincts is base. We may use them for base or sub-human purposes, but that is another matter. Our sexuality, far from being a lower and less worthy part of our human nature, is integral to it and therefore must be integrated into that search for union with God which is the end of all our being. The poet John Milton expresses something of our problem in the dialogue between Adam and the Archangel Raphael in *Paradise Lost*. Adam asks Raphael if the angels love and, if so, how they express it,

> . . . by looks only, or do they mix
> Irradiance, virtual or immediate touch?

Milton recounts the archangel's embarrassed answer:

95

A Priestless People?

To whom the angel with a smile that glowed
Celestial rosy red, love's proper hue,
Answered. Let it suffice thee that thou know'st
Us happy, and without love no happiness.

Many, I think, share Raphael's embarrassment in reconciling sexual feeling with their understanding of the spiritual life.

Fundamentally, that kind of religious embarrassment finds its source in the rejection of our humanity. It needs to be stressed in season and out of season that only by striving to be fully human can we hope to fulfil God's will for us. We are not meant to live like animals, noble as they are; but neither are we meant to live like angels, if indeed there are such. We are meant to live as human beings, creatures with minds and bodies, limbs and senses, feelings and sensuality, of the earth, earthy. The Bible creation myth makes our nature and therefore our dignity plain: 'God shaped *man from the soil of the ground*' (Genesis 2: 7): that phrase, 'man from the soil of the ground' is actually what the Hebrew word 'adamah' means. Genesis goes on to say of the man and woman thus created, that they are to find the deepest expression of their relationship, not in some ethereal spiritual union, but in the uniting of their flesh: 'they become one flesh'. The Bible is full of fleshly, bodily, earthly language. Psalm 22 may be taken as typical:

It was you who drew me from the womb
And soothed me on my mother's breast.

Jesus' own parables abound with allusions to everyday, earthly human life: a woman baking bread or frantically,

96

in her poverty, searching for a lost coin; a farmer sowing wheat or faced with possible bankruptcy because his business rival has sown darnel in his fields; a father having to come downstairs in the middle of the night because his improvident friend failed to reach the baker's before it shut; the young teenagers chosen to be bridesmaids excitedly awaiting the arrival of the groom. There is a warm and welcoming acceptance here of the details of human life, human life in its continuous drama of work, anxiety, love, impatience and excitement. The stories of Jesus' miracles breathe the same earthy humanness: extra wine, which is extra in quality too, is provided to keep the wedding party going; a son is restored to his heartbroken mother; a blind man is cured by having paste made from dust and spittle rubbed on his eyes.

None of this should surprise us. When God chose to reveal himself to us, he did so in a form utterly and completely human. John's Gospel tells us that 'the Word was made flesh'. The Greek term translated 'flesh' there is 'sarx', which means ordinary, everyday human flesh, flesh which feels cold and heat, which flushes red with excitement, pales with fear, sweats with heat, ripples with pleasure and shudders with horror; flesh with all the bodily functions that properly belong to it; flesh which warms to love and recoils from hate; flesh without which not one of us can call herself or himself a human being. God in Christ sets his seal upon the worth, the goodness and the dignity of the individual human person of flesh and blood, made from the earth, made to return to the earth and destined for glory in the resurrection of the body. Is this not what we all instinctively feel? Is this not the reason why we find the concept of a 'spiritual' life depressing? How damaging has been the division introduced between body and soul, with the soul seen as the prisoner of the body which can only be itself when released by death? If that were true, how could we say with sincerity that we believed in or looked forward to the resurrection of the body? Jesus is surely a better guide here than Plato. Does the doctrine of the Incarnation, which is at the centre of Christian belief, not teach us that all dogma is the recognition of the glory of being created human, all morality the effort to be fully human and all worship the celebration of our humanity? In the Eucharist, when we give thanks for Christ, we do so in the bodily words which Jesus himself gave us: this is my body; this is my blood. We are to rejoice not only in his body and blood, but in our own, but it is *our* own flesh and blood that he took in order to bring us to union with his Father.

We must face up to the consequences of these ideas in the way in which we regard our sexuality. That, too, is part of the flesh of which Jesus and all of us are made; if we ignore it, suppress it or even 'sublimate' it, that is, place it on so 'high' a plane that it becomes simply another way of ignoring its reality, we diminish ourselves as human beings and to that extent diminish the image of God within us. Genesis insists upon human sexuality in its first creation account: 'God created man in the image of himself, in the image of God he created him, male and female he created them.' The rhythm of the passage stresses the point. It does not simply *happen* that God created human beings (and incidentally, that is what the word 'man' means in the beginning of the text, God created man – the Hebrew is in the plural, meaning men and women) male and female; the sexual distinction is part of his plan in the beginning, part of what Matthew Fox wonderfully calls the original blessing bestowed upon us in our beginnings. This is confirmation in our foundation myth that our sexuality is a vital part of our humanness. Unless we exploit it to the full, then we shall never grow in holiness, which is of course the growth to wholeness.

I hope that no reader imagines that I am being so foolish as to propose a new religion of sex, in which overt and indiscriminate sexual activity becomes the expression of worship. Such ideas are essentially pagan, not Christian. Temple prostitutes were a feature of ancient Roman religion, and were so precisely because paganism denied the basic goodness and wholeness of human living. Once the dignity and value of a human being are recognized for their true worth as seen by God, he or she cannot be used for any purpose, even a religious one. Even Christianity has been slow to grasp this truth. It took the Church leadership 1800 years to reject slavery; that same leadership has still not rid itself of its innate tendency to diminish human sexuality. So, obviously, we are not preaching a doctrine of free sexual love for that would be to insult human beings, render sex meaningless and strew obstacles in the growth to wholeness. But it *does* mean that we need to relate to one another as human beings, as male or female human beings; and to recognize that we are a mixture of both. The character of our sexuality should not be taken simply from its physical manifestations; there is more of the male *and* female in the human psyche than perhaps we altogether realize. We need, I think, to explore our own being; we need, perhaps in prayer, to ask for the gift of self-knowledge so that we may approach both God and our fellow human beings in the fullness of our own selves, whatever that may be.

Our willingness to accept this, and to accept the sexual dimension which is an essential part of our human being, can perhaps be measured by our reaction to statements about the sexuality of Jesus. Scripture assures us that he was a man, human like us in all but sin: in *all* but sin. Yet, in practice, do we not feel uncomfortable at the suggestion that sexuality was part of his human being and even more uncomfortable at the suggestion that he experienced sexual feelings? If that is the case, then we have not really recognized our own sexuality as part of God's gracious gift in making us human beings. Our discomfort reveals our own misgivings about sexuality, our abiding belief that our ultimate vocation is to be angels – which is to contradict the Incarnation. We see this discomfort at work in the commentators' reaction to the seventeenth verse of the twentieth chapter of John's Gospel. This is the chapter which describes the meeting of Jesus and Mary Magdalene in the garden after the resurrection. It is a moving scene:

> As she said this, she turned round and saw Jesus standing there, though she did not realize that it was Jesus. Jesus said to her, 'Woman, why are you weeping? Who are you looking for?' Supposing him to be the gardener, she said, 'Sir, if you have taken him away, tell me where you have put him, and I will go and remove him.' Jesus said, 'Mary!' She turned round then and said to him in Hebrew, 'Rabbuni!' which means Master. Jesus said to her, 'Do not cling to me, because I have not yet ascended to the Father. But go and find my brothers, and tell

them: I am ascending to my Father and your Father, to my God and your God.' So Mary of Magdala told the disciples, 'I have seen the Lord,' and that he said these things to her.

John 20:14–18

Strange interpretations have been given of this passage, reflecting distorted views of both sex and women. Some commentators have suggested that Jesus was naked at the time, having left the grave clothes in the tomb and that is why Mary Magdalene first of all turned away and then was told by Jesus not to cling to him. Others have suggested that Thomas was told that he *should* touch Jesus' wounds because he was an important male apostle, whereas Mary was told she must not touch Jesus, because she was only a woman and had been a terrible sinner as well – for which, incidentally, there is no shred of evidence in the Gospels. Such aberrations or, indeed, any other exegesis is not my concern in this book. I refer to the passage because it reveals, simply and movingly, the view taken by the writer of Jesus' relationships with his friends. The author clearly saw nothing scandalous in the idea of Mary wanting to cling to Jesus. And Jesus is given no puritanical reply rebuking Mary. He is shown as saying that she should not cling to him because he has not yet ascended to the Father. This probably means that Jesus' resurrection is not meant to restore his former physical presence to his friends but has inaugurated an entirely new way of being with them, which will take place after the ascension in the bestowing of the Spirit. It is one of those ironies of the Church that the Latin version of Jesus' words, '*Noli tangere*', is the source of the phrase to which we earlier referred which has become the watchword summing up the need to preserve the citadel of priestly celibacy.

Jesus, in fact, had a far more tactile, emotional approach to people than we perhaps realize, than perhaps we would think 'nice' or proper. He laid hands on the sick; we are told that he loved Lazarus, Martha and Mary; that he conceived a great love for the rich young man; John is described as the disciple whom Jesus loved; Peter is asked three times if he loves him more than the others do, to make up for his denial; Jesus weeps over Jerusalem and over the death of Lazarus and takes little children in his arms. It would make a nonsense of the text, and ultimately of our belief in the Incarnation, if we took this to refer to some kind of transcendental, spiritual love of God for humankind: it is, if we are to believe in the Incarnation, the warm, human love of a man for other men and women, a love which is authentically and fully human.

Jesus is the ideal man. He was not afraid of his feelings; nor should we be. This does not, of course, mean that we can give them free rein. We must put a bridle on them; but the purpose of a bridle is not to prevent movement but to guide it, to ensure that the horse goes where we want it to go. The bridle we need to put on our feelings is the bridle of love. We must use our humanity, our sexuality, for the expression of love, which is always – as St Paul reminds us in the glorious thirteenth chapter of Corinthians – the seeking of the good of the other.

To say this is often to invite the charge of laxity, of making things too easy: we must have rules, we are told. But love is *the* rule for the Christian. We have seen the ineffectiveness of other rules. Has the rule-bound approach prevented adultery, fornication, perversion, child abuse, incest and the 1001 other sexual sins listed in all their detail in the heavy tomes of our moral theologians? To ask the question is to answer it. It is *just* possible that a morality, a sexual morality, built on genuine love would achieve more for God's kingdom.

If any reader feels that we are here taking an extreme position in the celebration of our humanness and the sexuality built in to our humanness, we can only answer that this seems to be God's view of his creation. Read the words of the rapturous love-song in the Bible, the Song of Songs, the love-song which centuries of scandalized spiritual and ascetic theology tried to pretend was an account of a purely spiritual relationship between God and the soul. We must never disregard the significance of the fact that the inspired scriptural writer chose the language of overtly sexual love. The girl, for instance, speaks in the ecstasy of her love:

> Draw me in your footsteps, let us run.
> The king has brought me into his rooms;
> you will be our joy and our gladness.
> we shall praise your love more than wine;
> how right it is to love you.
>
> My love is a sachet of myrrh
> lying between my breasts.
>
> How beautiful you are, my beloved,
> and how you delight me!
> Our bed is the greensward.
>
> He has taken me to his cellar,
> and his banner over me is love.
> Feed me with raisin cakes,

restore me with apples,
for I am sick with love.

On my bed at night I sought
the man who is my sweetheart . . .
when I found my sweetheart,
I caught him, would not let him go,
not till I had brought him
to my mother's house,
to the room where she conceived me!

Let my love come into his garden,
let him taste its most exquisite fruits.

The lover responds:

I come into my garden,
my sister, my promised bride,
I pick my myrrh and balsam,
I eat my honey and my honeycomb,
I drink my wine and milk.

He concludes the poem:

Set me like a seal on your heart,
like a seal on your arm.
For love is strong as Death,
passion as relentless as Sheol.
The flash of it is a flash of fire,
A flame of Yahweh himself.
Love no flood can quench,
no torrents drown.
Were a man to offer all his family wealth

to buy love,
contempt is all he would gain.

In this tender, sensuous, vibrant expression and celebration
of sexual love and of human sexuality, the Word of God
speaks to the heart of each one of us, priest and lay person
alike. This is not to prove that every priest *ought* to be
married. It certainly suggests, however, that no harm will
be done to his priesthood if he is.

8

The Meaning of the Mass

Then they told their story of what had happened
on the road and how they had recognized him
at the breaking of bread.

(Luke 24:35)

The high regard in which the priest has been traditionally
held by Catholics is undoubtedly in large measure due to
his being seen as having the power to say Mass, in which
he changes bread and wine into the Body and Blood of
Jesus Christ. This is, however, to ascribe to the priest a
status beyond what the New Testament warrants. The position of the priest in the constitution of the Church will be
considered in more detail in the next chapter. Here, it will
be useful to review our understanding of the Mass. Popular
Catholicism embodies two ideas about the Mass: one, by
coming to Mass we are engaged upon the formal, public
worship of God; two, the most important thing about the
Mass itself is that through the action of the priest Christ
is made really present in the Eucharist, so that we can
receive his Body and Blood in Holy Communion as the
spiritual nourishment of our souls. Certainly, such ideas
underlay much of my own early Catholic education.

The fact is that both of these ideas would have been
puzzling to the first Christians. In the beginning, they made

The Meaning of the Mass

quite a clear distinction between worship and the celebration of the Eucharist. According to the Acts of the Apostles, the disciples 'went as a body to the Temple every day but met in their houses for the breaking of bread' (2:46). Texts like this, especially Paul's remarks in 1 Corinthians 11, where he rebukes the Christians for turning the celebration of the Eucharist into a selfish social gathering, show that the first disciples, the ones closest to Jesus, thought of the Eucharist primarily in community terms: community with Christ and, in him, community with each other.

The Eucharist in the beginning, therefore, was primarily a community celebration. Jewish religious history and also Jewish social custom shed light on the character of this community celebration. The foundation belief of the Jewish people was that they were bound together in a special relationship with God: God had made them his own people by means of a special agreement or covenant. Once they had become established in Palestine, they began to celebrate the setting up of that covenant with God in their annual Passover meal.

In celebrating that anniversary meal, the Jews looked to the past, the present and the future. They thanked God for what he had done for them in the past; they renewed their confidence that God was still acting for them in the present; and they looked forward to a future in which their people would become sharers in a new and everlasting covenant between God and themselves.

As Christians, we believe that this new and everlasting covenant is fundamentally established by the coming of Jesus, the Christ. But the first Christians did not, upon being baptized, think of themselves as having adopted a religion essentially different from what they had believed in before: 'Christian' was a nickname given them by others, not taken for themselves. Acts 11:26 tells us that 'It was at Antioch that the disciples were first called "Christian"'. The Gentiles had obviously derived the term from their mistaken belief that 'Christ' was a name instead of a title meaning 'anointed'. They thought of themselves as the Jews who had been faithful to God's promise. It was inevitable, therefore, that they should see what Jesus had done for them in terms of their religious history, and especially in terms of their original great deliverance from Egypt: the Exodus. This is rather as we British people tend to see all our national deliverances now as another Dunkirk. In consequence, they transferred the language and imagery of the Exodus to their understanding of the saving work of Christ. Under the leadership of Moses, their faithful ancestors had passed from political, material and religious slavery in Egypt to freedom in their own land. The religious festival commemorating the Exodus was called the 'passover'. Now, under the leadership of Jesus, who was regarded as the new Moses (a particular feature of Matthew's Gospel), God's faithful people once again pass over from slavery to freedom; but this time it is from the slavery of sin and death to the freedom of grace and eternal life through the death and resurrection of Jesus. A major part of the meaning of the Christian Eucharist is that it is the religious action which celebrates this passover.

This point is heavily emphasized in the accounts of the Last Supper given to us by Mark, Matthew and Luke. Christian tradition, aided by Leonardo da Vinci's famous painting which places the disciples with Jesus on a bench on just one side of the table, has quite firmly established in our minds that the Last Supper was the first Eucharist.

The Meaning of the Mass

It is salutary to remember that the synoptic gospels insist that what Jesus and his disciples were actually engaged in at the time was celebrating the Jewish Passover meal. Mark, Matthew and Luke wanted their readers to link that particular meal firmly with the *ancient* covenant between God and the people of Israel.

These Gospels tell us that, during this meal, Jesus announced the establishment of the new covenant, in his body and blood. Once they had become convinced that Jesus had risen from the dead, the disciples came to realize one of the meanings of the supper which they had celebrated. Jesus had accomplished his own passage from death to life through his crucifixion and resurrection: his body had been broken and his blood shed on the cross; God raised him to life in the body on the third day after. So, by eating the bread and drinking the wine which Jesus himself had set apart and had *consecrated* as the truly effective sign of his very body and blood surrendered for them, the believers realized that they were expressing their will to be united as closely as possible to him in his passage through death to life. Moreover, since this ritual was established by Jesus, the participants had faith that Jesus would in fact bring about that unity with him.

For this reason, Paul and Luke show Jesus describing his blood as the blood of the *new* covenant: through Moses, God had bound his people to himself in a special relationship whereby they were to be his own people; now, through Christ, God covenants to establish a new relationship by which *all* are able to become children of God and sisters and brothers of Christ, through the power of the Holy Spirit. By eating and drinking the sacrament of the Lord's body and blood, believers manifested both their desire to participate in this covenant *and* their faith that Christ has indeed incorporated them into it.

We must never lose sight of the deeply Jewish background to these events. When the Jews of the Old Testament, that is, of the *old* covenant, celebrated their Passover meal, they did not imagine that they were simply thinking about the past, like old soldiers recalling their memories of battles fought long ago. They believed that participation in the meal did, there and then, give them a share in God's saving actions: they were inserted into his plans for the world. It was in that same spirit that the first Christians believed that their celebration of the meal of the new covenant *really* inserted them into God's saving plan for humanity in Christ.

Because this is the very essence of the eucharistic celebration, it holds true for what we are supposed to be doing at Mass nowadays. When we come to Mass, we are recalling with gratitude ('eukaristia' in Greek, *eucharist* in English), what God has already done for us in Christ; we reaffirm our desire as a community to persevere in the present in this new life of union with God and with one another; and we look forward to the future, to the full and final establishment of the Kingdom. These are the ideas which are set out in our various forms of the long, eucharistic prayer which forms the backbone of the Mass ceremony.

To leave matters there would be to oversimplify. We must also take into account the factor of Jewish social history. The Passover meal was celebrated only once a year; Mass is celebrated at least every Sunday. It is clear from the New Testament that the early eucharistic celebrations were also weekly events, held now on the day of the

Lord, Sunday, not the Sabbath. There must have been more here, then, than a 'Christianization', so to speak, of the Jewish Passover festival. This becomes even more obvious when we look at John's Gospel. John's account of the Last Supper is quite different from that of the synoptics. It describes in detail Jesus washing the feet of his disciples and Judas' treachery; then it switches to the long discourse of Jesus to his disciples, which is generally regarded as the fruit of the Joannine community's meditations on memories of Jesus' conversations with his disciples. There is no description of the meal, but according to John, whatever meal was eaten was certainly not the Passover meal, for he makes it quite clear that when the Jews brought Jesus before the Roman authorities, they had not yet celebrated the Passover.

Our understanding of Jewish ritual meals of the time can help resolve this apparent discrepancy and also deepen our understanding of what we are doing when we celebrate the Eucharist. We are all quite familiar with the notion of ritual meals in a perfectly non-religious context, ranging from the old-fashioned Sunday family lunch to monthly meetings in the United States of organizations such as the Water Buffaloes Club. But we are perhaps less familiar with the fact that nearly *every* Jewish meal was a religious ritual meal with quite formal observance of the rules. It always began with a prayer of thanksgiving, rather more elaborate than our Grace. Bread was broken and shared at the beginning and there was a blessing each time the wine cup was refilled. There was usually a longer prayer of thanksgiving at the end of the meal. The prayers and blessings varied according to the character of the celebration. The Passover meal fitted neatly into this system, since it was a major annual ritual meal with very special blessings and prayers. But it was not the only such meal. And while, as we have seen, Mark, Matthew and Luke were obviously very anxious to associate the meaning of the Passover with the Eucharist, it is easy to see why the first Christians saw no reason to limit their celebration of the Eucharist to an annual event only. Every time they met as a community in Christ's name, they would feel it natural to share in a meal in which they gave thanks for all that God had done for them through him.

The various 'parts' of the Mass find their meaning and place in relation to this overall scheme. For example, the readings from scripture correspond to the use made by the Jews of the scriptures in their ritual meals, especially the Passover. At that celebration, such readings enriched the participants' memories through hearing again the sacred records of God's dealings with them. We Christians have inherited all that God promised to them, and more; the record of that inheritance is enshrined in the Bible. There can hardly be a fitter time in which to become familiar with that record than during our celebration of all that God, in his goodness and mercy, has given us. It would also be a good time for any particular community to hear messages from other Christian communities, and especially from individual Christians like Paul who had founded their particular 'church'.

The Prayer of the Faithful (or the Bidding Prayers) has its place in the Mass for the same basic reason. This is the community prayer for the particular needs of the whole People of God, of the world, of the local community and of the individual. The Mass is the community of God's people at prayer in Christ, a community which needs to remember in God's presence its local and material needs, as well as its universal and spiritual ones.

The money collection is a memory, rather more vividly preserved in our harvest festivals, of the ancient offertory procession when gifts for the sick, the aged and poor in the community were brought to the Communion table for later distribution. It is sad that the development of the Church has in effect turned such giving into support and maintenance of our own ever-growing material plant and structure.

It is, too, this notion of community which explains the little ceremony in which, before receiving Communion, those present exchange a sign of peace and friendship with one another. We are gathered together, not as individuals, but as a community, the community of God's people; his family, as sisters and brothers in Christ. In receiving Holy Communion, we of course demonstrate our desire for the closest possible union with Christ. But that union with him is wholly dependent upon our being in loving union with one another: and human nature requires some external sign of that union – although, obviously, it is an empty mockery if we are not *really* trying to behave as a loving community.

At the beginning of this chapter, I observed that the first Christians seem to have made a distinction between worship and the celebration of the Eucharist. But as Christianity developed, and especially after the destruction of the Temple in Jerusalem, it grew further and further away from its Jewish roots and eventually became a distinct religion. It was natural, therefore, that the memorial meal of the Eucharist should also form the expression of Christian worship of God in the name of Jesus. After all, as we recall all that God has done for us in Christ, we are inevitably moved to gratitude, to wonder and to praise – in other words, to worship. When we come to Mass, then, we are indeed engaged upon the public worship of God. But it is vital that we also remember that we are worshipping as a community, bound to God by the Body broken and Blood shed of Christ, that body and blood raised to eternal life by God the Father in the power of the Spirit.

Catholic theology has traditionally described the Mass as a sacrifice. This could be a misleading term if it causes us to think simply of blood offerings and animal slaughter. We also think of 'making sacrifices' in the sense of the heroic bearing of hardship. Such conceptions are not easily compatible with notions of celebration. Undue emphasis on the sacrificial aspect of the Mass has also, in the past, led to the horrendous theological conclusion that a wrathful God had insisted upon the violent punishment of his son in order to assuage his anger and his outraged justice. It is perhaps more helpful to remember that essentially sacrifice means 'making holy': Jesus has made all existence holy through his Incarnation. Through the Eucharist we symbolize, celebrate and effect our agreement with that. Sacrifice does also, of course, mean *offering*, and we can rightly say that Jesus offered himself to the Father on the cross because his death was the direct result of his total commitment to his Father. If he had been less loyal, his enemies would have had no reason to get rid of him. It is the whole of Jesus' work that we celebrate and commemorate in the Eucharist, it is that total work into which we are inserted in the celebration, and therefore we can rightly be said to be offering Jesus' sacrifice with him.

Another aspect of ordinary Catholic eucharistic teaching

The Meaning of the Mass

which easily leads to misunderstanding is the concept of Transubstantiation. Not all Catholics realize that this word is only a label – it is *not* the reality of the doctrine. The Council of Trent, which set out the Roman Catholic Church's official position with regard to matters disputed or denied by the sixteenth-century Reformers, refers to it like this:

> If anyone denies that in the most holy sacrament of the Eucharist there is that wonderful and singular change of the whole substance of bread into the body and the whole substance of wine into the blood of Jesus Christ, leaving only the appearance of bread and wine, which change indeed the Catholic Church aptly calls transubstantiation, let him be accursed.
>
> (Declaration 884, *Enchiridion Symbolorum*
> Denzinger, op. cit., p. 309)

In other words, the *doctrine* is about contemporary Catholic understanding of the nature of the eucharistic elements after the words of consecration in the Mass, and 'transubstantiation' is simply the term which the Council of Trent thought apt to express it. It does not, therefore, rule out the possibility of some more apt word to be used in other circumstances. And there is no doubt that other circumstances have indeed arisen.

It is important to recognize that the Council of Trent's definitions were framed against the background of Aristotelian philosophy. This reckoned that it was possible to distinguish in every object between its accidents and its substance. The accidents were all the sense-perceptible properties like colour, shape, weight and so on. So, apples are red, green or yellow, are of different sizes and have various flavours. Yet, they are all apples; they all possess the substance, the reality, of appleness. The Church Fathers were saying that in the case of the Eucharist, these external properties – the accidents – remained, but the substance which they indicated – bread and wine – had now given way to another substance, the body and blood of Christ, which were not expressed by their normal accidents. Clearly, Aristotelian philosophy is no longer an adequate vehicle for conveying our understanding of reality but it is not so easy to find a suitable substitute. And perhaps it is not a useful search anyway. All Christians, surely, are agreed that Jesus told his disciples that the bread and wine were his body and blood; John 6 preserves a clear realization by his followers that he really meant what he said. Moreover, Protestant reaction against Roman Catholic doctrine was really a reaction against what seemed to them to be the idea that Jesus was *physically* present in the Eucharist, which of course is no part of official Catholic teaching, although it has to be admitted that such ideas have often crept into popular piety.

Perhaps it would be more profitable for us to concentrate on the celebration of the Eucharist as an *action* which we perform in memory of Jesus rather than to spend fruitless time on trying to explain *how* he is present. Indeed, over-concern with this aspect of the Eucharist has undoubtedly led to neglect of the importance of the presence of Jesus, no less real, in other ways in his Church: through the preaching of God's Word, for instance, or in the assembly of the faithful gathered to celebrate and commemorate his life, death and resurrection.

Readers can hardly have failed to notice that this description of what we are doing at Mass has made little mention of the priest. This does not mean that the priest is unimportant. All celebrations require someone to preside to ensure the orderliness and effectiveness of the proceedings. When such celebrations are indicative of the fundamental character and purpose of the celebrating group, it is obviously important that the one presiding has the necessary authority to represent the group and to ensure the validity of its proceedings. But none of this should blind us to the essential fact that it is the *community* as a whole which is celebrating.

To sum up: at the Last Supper, Jesus gave to his followers his body to eat and his blood to drink, under the sign of bread and wine. He told them that they were to continue this action in his memory, as an effective sign of their union with him, and in him, of their union with each other, and finally, by the power of the Spirit, of their union in him with God the Father. It is the *whole* Church which carries out this celebration, it is not an action performed by the priest with the faithful in pious and humble attendance. The priest is the president of a celebrating community which is gathered in order to deepen that union with God and one another, precisely *as* the Spirit-filled community redeemed by Christ and destined for glory with him. The priest is not an isolated mystical figure placed over and against that community. It is perhaps the failure fully to grasp the implications of this truth which has paralysed the search for imaginative solutions to the vocations crisis. Consequently, in the next chapter, I shall examine a little more fully the nature of the worshipping community and of the ordained priest's relationship to it.

9

The Essence of Ministerial Priesthood

You are a chosen race, a kingdom of priests.
(1 Peter 2:9)

Readers who have persevered this far may judge that the solution to the vocations crisis is the repeal of compulsory celibacy for priests. Such a reform, however valuable a contribution to the solution and however necessary on other grounds, would not, I believe, of itself remedy the real disease at the heart of the Church's life. Not every Church which permits its ministers to marry is over-supplied with clergy. Nor is there a dramatic shortage of candidates for the priesthood in every seminary throughout the world. Some parts of the Catholic world, particularly where social conditions are poor or which have been largely untouched by Vatican II reforms, can still furnish high seminary attendance figures. What is needed is not simply the repeal of the law but a change of heart and mind in those who sincerely believe that this law is good both for the ministerial priesthood and for the Church. To achieve this, we need to take a close look at our understanding of Christian priesthood itself.

No one denies that the priesthood is at the service of

the Church. Pope John Paul II devoted particular attention to this aspect of priesthood in his 1995 Maundy Thursday address to priests. So we ought to begin our examination of priesthood by reminding ourselves what the Church is *for*. The Church, the community of the People of God, exists solely that Christ may continue to be given to the world. Jesus is a living reality for millions, both now and during ages past, only because of the abiding commitment to him of so many faithful Christians down the centuries. Each successive age can have faith in Jesus, can love and reverence him as the pattern and meaning of their lives, only because of the existing community of those held together, however slenderly, by that same love and reverence. Our faith in Jesus is possible only because of the community which lives by faith in Jesus. That is the debt every believing Christian owes to the Church. And that Church does not exist apart from the believing Christians who constitute its membership.

In the Catholicism which has become the norm especially since mediaeval times, it has been customary to say that this is the reason why Jesus founded the Church. But this is a statement which needs some qualification. The New Testament does not show Jesus 'founding' a Church in the same way as William Booth founded the Salvation Army or Baden-Powell and his wife founded the Boy Scouts and Girl Guides. We naturally think of Christianity in general, and the Catholic Church in particular, as a new 'religion' founded by Jesus Christ. This is not the view of the New Testament writers, the first people to interpret the meaning of Christ's life for us. They did not see Jesus as the founder of a Church. In fact, the Gospels show Jesus using the word 'Church' only once, in the famous text: 'Thou art

Peter and on this rock I will build my Church' (see Matthew 16:13–20).

The vast amount of controversy and the extent of variation in the interpretation of this text, even inside the Roman Catholic Church, let alone among eminent biblical scholars outside it, make the passage of very uncertain value in determining Jesus' views on the structure of any society which would claim him as its founder. We cannot simply gloss over the fact that none of the other Gospels, including the other two synoptic gospels (Mark and Luke) which *do* record – though in less spectacular terms – Peter's confession of faith, knows anything of such a promise by Jesus. At the very least this demonstrates that Peter's position did not have the particular kind of importance for first-generation Christians which it came to possess for Catholics. It also raises the question as to whether Jesus actually made such a promise or whether we have here another stage in the development of the Matthean community's understanding of Jesus' intentions. It hardly needs to be added that this understanding did not envisage for Peter the position with its detailed powers now claimed for the Bishop of Rome. We must also remember that Matthew's Gospel was written within the context of the already existing Church; it stemmed from a Christian tradition strongly imbued with a sense of the community of Christ's followers as the new Israel, the new assembly of God's people.

The vision of the first Christians in general was much more Christ-centred than Church-centred. They saw Jesus as bringing to humankind, especially to the poor and oppressed of humankind, the life, love and freedom of God. Certainly, they described the results of this coming as the Kingdom of God. They clearly expected that the establishment of the Kingdom would mean the establishment of love, justice and peace on earth, based on a true brotherly and sisterly love among human beings under the universal fatherhood and motherhood of the God revealed most fully in Jesus. The Dominican theologian, Schillebeeckx, in his book, *The Church with a Human Face*, puts it like this: 'This gives rise among men and women to a new relationship to God, and the comprehensible and visible side of this new relationship is a new type of relationship among men and women within a community of peace, which brings liberation and opens up communication.'

The plain truth is that there was no 'ecclesiastical community', no Church that is, until the followers of Jesus came to believe in his resurrection. The Church arose from the binding together in the Spirit of those who believed in and proclaimed the resurrection of their crucified Lord. They were brought into fellowship by their common belief in and their commitment to Jesus, acknowledged now as conqueror of sin and Lord of life. The community consisted of those who declared themselves for Christ. The foundation members of the community had known and experienced Jesus himself; some of them committed to writing certain basic facts of that knowledge and experience, combined with their understanding in the light of their belief in the resurrection of the *meaning* of those facts and that experience, in what we have come to call the New Testament. Because the New Testament is the record of that foundation faith, it must remain the irreplaceable norm for all subsequent faith. But it is useful to remind ourselves that the New Testament came from the community, and not the community from the New Testament.

A Priestless People?

We shall, therefore, have a better idea of the nature of the Church if we begin with the circumstances which gave it birth, rather than by an examination of some external constitution imposed, so to speak, from 'outside' the Church. It is true that the first members of this community-coming-to-be certainly structured it in accordance with their understanding of Jesus' mission. In *that* sense, of course, it is true to say that Jesus founded the 'Church'. But that is a very different reality from the notion of a society directly founded by Jesus and equipped by him with a constitution, regulations and officials. All that administrative apparatus came from the community and not from detailed dispositions made by Jesus himself.

The direct circumstances of the Church's birth were belief in the risen Christ and a conviction that God had summoned those who held this belief to proclaim him to the rest of humankind. This was seen as the Christ-given task of *all* its members. They believed that the Spirit had been given to all of them for the accomplishment of this glorious task. Jesus' resurrection from the dead convinced them that death and therefore sin and all its consequences were no longer the last word in human affairs. Life, freedom, lasting love and joy were really on offer to men and women and the first believers saw their mission as making this Good News available to the world. That was the priestly (that is, sanctifying) task of the whole community.

Before all else, therefore, the Church is at the service of humankind to further Christ's cause in the world, not to ensure its own constitution and structure. It is Christ's cause which is the sole criterion of the validity of its declarations, doctrines, regulations and organization.

The Essence of Ministerial Priesthood

Anything it does or says which hinders Christ's cause in the world cannot come from the Spirit of Christ; it cannot be authentically Christian. And in particular the Church, and especially its leadership and officials, need to be constantly aware that they are in no way an end in themselves. The Church is always a signpost, never a destination. The Church is the vehicle and not the purpose of the Incarnation.

The Second Vatican Council expressed this vividly in its description of the Church as the People of God. The importance which the Council attached to this concept of the Church is shown by the fact that it devoted to it the whole of Chapter II in its decree, *Lumen Gentium* (Light of the Nations), on the nature of the Church. This description of the Church marked a welcome return to the New Testament conception of the Church as the community of people called together by God in Christ for his saving purpose. We believe that a full grasp of the implications of this title, 'The People of God', can take us far along the road to solving the vocations crisis.

Most Catholics, in practice, speak about the Church as an entity distinct from themselves. They do not think of themselves as actually *being* the Church. They tend, indeed, to identify the Church with only a section of it, usually the officials within it or the authorities over it. So, for example, you hear the expression 'the Church teaches this' or 'the Church believes that', when what is really meant is that the authorities in the Church teach this or believe that. One hopes, of course, that in practice the authorities would not believe one thing and the people another, but the distinction is possible and has been verified, in fact increasingly so in our own day. We need to be quite clear that we can speak with complete accuracy of 'the Church' only if the expression, 'the people of God', can be adequately substituted for it. The first letter of Peter is explicit:

> But you are a chosen race, a kingdom of priests, a holy nation, a people to be a personal possession to sing the praises of God who called you out of the darkness into his wonderful light. Once you were a non-people and now you are the People of God (1 Peter 2:9–10).

Certain extremely important practical conclusions for our lives as Christian members of our various communities follow from this. One such conclusion is that we must, in practice as well as in theory, recognize that there is a fundamental equality of all members of the Church: some are not more members than others; some, as it were, more deeply baptized than others; some called to a greater degree of commitment than others. We noted earlier that Jesus' call, 'You are to be perfect as your heavenly Father is perfect' (Matthew 5:48), was addressed to *all* his followers and not simply to a select group among them. There can be, then, no question of a Church which exists 'over there', apart from all the baptized, or of a Church in which some are more equal than others. The first Christians were not interested in questions of rank: how could they be when they believed that the Spirit of God was not interested in them either? Acts 2:17–18 has Peter declaring to the Jews in the Lord's name,

> I shall pour out my Spirit on all humanity.
> Your sons and daughters shall prophesy,
> your young people shall see visions,
> your old people dream dreams.

> Even on the slaves, men and women,
> shall I pour out my Spirit.

The sense of equality among believers is echoed for example in 2 Corinthians 5:17: 'So for *anyone* who is in Christ, there is a new creation: the old order is gone and a new being is there to see' and, famously, in Galatians 3:26–28:

> ... every one of you that has been baptized has been clothed in Christ. There can be neither Jew nor Greek, there can be neither slave nor freeman, there can be neither male nor female – for you are all one in Christ Jesus.

Resounding through all these and similar texts is the spirit of the passage from Matthew (23:8–12) who has Jesus declaring to his followers,

> You, however, must not allow yourselves to be called Rabbi since you have only one Master, and you are all brothers. You must call no one on earth your father, since you have only one Father, and he is in heaven. Nor must you allow yourselves to be called teachers, for you have only one Teacher, the Christ.

Christian baptism was clearly believed to bring into existence a new creation in which our customary religious and social opposing distinctions are quite simply abolished.

Hence, there should simply be no room in the true Church of Christ for clerical monopoly or privilege. The laity's share in the essential work of the Church is theirs by right, not by privilege or delegation. If by excluding lay people from certain functions for no other reason than that they are lay the mission of the Church to bring Christ to the world is hindered or jeopardized, then such exclusion cannot be justified from the Gospel. This surely is an essential principle in coming to any proper understanding of the true nature of priesthood.

Catholics tend to become nervous when they hear this kind of statement. This is because we have all become very used to the present organization and structure of the Church. It is very easy to take for granted that how things are now is how they have always been. But this is not so. Many, if not most, Catholics have a mental picture, inherited from their schooldays and from sermons, of Jesus going about his work in a highly organized way, with a clear blueprint of the institution he had in mind for bringing his projects to fruition. We think of him systematically choosing, after due prayer and consideration, 12 men whom he would send out (this is the basic meaning of 'apostle', one sent out) in his name and endowed with his power. These men he is said to have ordained as 'priests', exactly as in our sense of the word, at the 'Last Supper' when they were told to do 'this', that is, what he had just done, in memory of him. Moreover, these newly created 'priests' described as having been directly 'ordained' by Jesus were not simply priests: they are said to have been 'bishops' and therefore possessing the power to ordain other priests. This they proceeded to do; some of the priests they ordained were in their turn made bishops and so were able to hand on the priestly line right down to the present day.

This popular notion simply does not correspond to what

is written in the New Testament. To be sure, the evidence is strong that Jesus did choose 12 men as his special helpers and that these men were called, though not exclusively so, apostles. It is, however, possible that it was the first Christian converts from Judaism rather than Jesus himself who fixed on the idea of a nucleus of 12 in order to express their notion of the Church as the new Israel developing from the ancient 12 tribes of Israel.

However that may be, there is certainly no suggestion that these men were priests in our sense. In fact, all the evidence points to the exact opposite. The New Testament writers scrupulously avoid calling them, or any other individual disciple of Jesus, a priest. It is strange that official Catholic teaching – for example, in the new Catechism – does not advertise this fact. But ignoring what the New Testament has to say about priesthood will not alter what is in the New Testament. There is a tendency to assume that the officials in the Christian community to whom the New Testament does refer are in fact 'priests' as we understand that function now. But this is a false assumption. Edmund Hill OP, in his book, *Ministry and Authority in the Catholic Church*, describes the reality of the situation with his usual succinctness: 'The Latin and Greek respectively for what we now nearly always mean by "priest" are *sacerdos* and *hiereus*; and the word "priest" is correctly used in English translations of the Bible for these words, and for the Hebrew, *kohen*. And the point is . . . that in the New Testament the people called *presbyteri* (priests) and the people called *episcopi* (bishops) and the people called *diaconi* (deacons) are never called *sacerdotes* or *hiereis* (priests). Absolutely never. Not a single time' (pp. 56–7). In fact the *only* persons described in the

New Testament as priests are Jesus himself and all the faithful.

This is not of itself to devalue the current official Roman Catholic understanding of priesthood. It is simply to make clear that this understanding can in no way be described as a *continuation* of a New Testament priesthood. Priesthood is seen now as the exclusive prerogative of a male whose 'ordination' has endowed him within his very being with powers to perform certain actions which the lay members of the Church do not have and which laywomen can never have. The most important of these 'powers' are to consecrate bread and wine so that they become truly the Body and Blood of Jesus, and to absolve from sin. The belief in the possession of such powers by these privileged persons has led to the concentration of all ruling power in the hands of this clerical élite.

We shall never deal successfully with the problems which today beset the ministry in the Roman Catholic Church, until the fact is openly faced that the current Catholic conception of priesthood, as summarized here, is *not* a New Testament blueprint but a development from those times. It has been extremely damaging to the Church that this development has not taken place within an overall understanding of priesthood as a gift to the whole Church. It has brought about the absurd situation that whole communities of believing Christians across the world have been deprived of the Eucharist because there are insufficient men coming forward to fulfil the Roman authorities' criteria for a valid Eucharist. Laymen, and even laywomen, are now permitted to lead the prayers and readings at Christian worship and to distribute pre-consecrated bread in Holy Communion. In some parts, they are even permitted to recite the scriptural narrative of institution of the Eucharist. But the actual grace of celebrating the Eucharist 'live', so to speak, which is at the heart of the Church's life and which brings Christ to his people in a very special way, is forbidden unless a man who conforms, not to the openness of the Gospel but to the narrow requirements of ecclesiastical canon law, is present to say the special words.

I have been at pains to stress that the Mass is the action of the whole community indwelt by the Spirit under the presidency of the celebrant. We need to beware of giving any impression, to ourselves as much as to others, that it is a quasi-magical rite which produces its effects altogether independently of the dispositions and commitment of all the participants. It is *that* truth which the practice of the Church must safeguard and not some legal requirement imposed in isolation from the reality of the worshipping community.

This is not to say that within the Church everyone ought to be allowed to do everything. For the sake of good order and harmony within the Church, there is a strong case for reserving certain functions to particular people. As Ambrosiaster, an early Christian commentator on *The Letter to the Hebrews*, recognized: 'When all do everything, that is irrational, vulgar and abhorrent.' In ordinary circumstances, it is clearly right and good to reserve presiding at the Eucharist to a person recognized by the community as having that function. The damage to the Church has come from the belief that the *reason* for that reservation is not the Christian good of the community but that the person so designated has an innate, almost ontological, power to perform actions denied to the rest of the baptized. The Vatican insists, and had its insistence included in the

Vatican II documents, that there is a difference of kind as well as degree between the priesthood of the ordained and that of all the faithful. We must honestly face the fact, and examine the consequences of the fact, that the New Testament lends no support to this distinction. On the contrary, the New Testament documents and the practice of the early Christians show that the Church felt sure that its Lord had left the community free to develop the exercise of the priesthood conferred upon the Church as a whole in whatever way best promoted Christ's purposes for his Church. Unfortunately, as Edward Schillebeeckx has observed in *The Church with a Human Face*, 'adaptations of a religion to its cultural environment which are often unavoidable in cultural terms are often given a subsequent religious legitimation' (p. 69).

It would be foolish to imagine that the first Christians held the naive belief that there was therefore no need for leadership or authority, structure or organization within the community which they had begun to form. No human society can survive without organization and authority. But they did recognize that theirs was an entirely new type of society. Jesus had provided them with the basic principles for the structuring of this society. The shocking character of the words is solid reason for supposing that they are his own:

> You know that among the gentiles the rulers lord it over them, and their great men make their authority felt. Among you this is not to happen. No; anyone who wants to become great among you must be your servant, and anyone who wants to be first among you must be your slave, just as the Son of Man came not to be

served but to serve, and to give his life as a ransom for many.

(Matthew 20:25-28.)

Jesus was not simply saying that those exercising authority among his followers were to do so kindly and justly: this is an obligation for *any* authority. He was instituting a new kind of authority, an authority of pure service. Slaves are not bearers of authority in any conventional sense, yet these are the persons offered as models for leaders among Jesus' disciples. Clearly, he intended something rather more realistic than the carved lettering in St Peter's which, more in aspiration than actuality, describes the Pope as 'Servant of the servants of God'.

The first Christians took Jesus at his word. A sense of freedom and of mutual service was the hallmark of the first communities which quickly followed the spread of belief in the resurrection of Jesus from the dead. Such communities taken together were known as the 'ekklesia', which we translate now as 'Church'. This was not a term coined by the Christians. It was already in use to describe the assembly of free, male citizens of a town or city called together to hold elections. The Christian assembly, however, was inspired less by this political model than by the Old Testament notion of the 'Assembly of the Lord'. In the early years there was no strict definition of the term. It could describe, for instance, the Christians freely gathered together in a particular house or act as a generic term for all such house communities in a given place. For example, Paul tells the Christians in Corinth the arrangements for the 'Church in Jerusalem' – they are to do the same as for 'the Churches in Galatia' (1 Corinthians 16:1). Romans

16:3 – 5 provides a wonderful example of this usage: Paul sends his greetings to Prisca and Aquila, his fellow workers in Christ Jesus, who risked their lives to save his. He sends to them thanks, not only from himself, but from *all the churches among the Gentiles* and sends his greetings *to the church at their house*. The first Christians, therefore, clearly regarded themselves as belonging to a group with not only local but also national and universal links.

It is therefore perfectly accurate to say that the Church began as a set of Christian house communities. Naturally enough, their basic structure was similar to that in civil society, that is, the household, which extended to everyone living in the 'house'. In these Christian households, preaching and instruction were provided and the Eucharist was celebrated. Obviously, the houses themselves were owned by the wealthy, but all the evidence shows that the participants in the life of such communities came from every level of society. There was, however, one extremely important distinction between the Christian household and that of civil, secular society. In the latter, the father – the 'paterfamilias' – exercised personal authority within a hierarchical structure. The first Christians took a conscious decision to depart from this approach. Schillebeeckx says that 'early Christianity was a brotherhood and sisterhood of equal partners' created through their baptism in the Spirit. They understood this to be fundamental to the nature of their association in Christ.

As we have already noted, these purely local groupings were sharply aware of their wider, even universal, connections. Although each household saw itself as 'the Church' in that place, its members were neither so foolish nor so narrow as to imagine that they constituted the whole

Church. They recognized the presence and envisaged the growth of a wider ecclesial community which would embrace these individual constituent churches without devouring them. For their structural model, they looked to the 'colleges' or 'free associations' existing in their Graeco-Roman world. One pagan writer actually describes a Christian house group as 'the college which is at the house of Sergia Paulina'. Such associations were characterized by considerable autonomy, but their members realized the need for an overall structure, if only at the very least to settle conflict and disputes. This was, of course, to be formed on the lines set out by Jesus in Matthew 20.

The so-called 'Council of Jerusalem' provides a good example of how this 'authority structure' operated in practice. A dispute had arisen among the Christians about the terms upon which Gentiles (non-Jews) could be accepted into the Church. Paul was the champion of those who denied that adherence to the Law of Moses was a necessary part of those terms. According to Galatians 2:2, Paul – but, according to Acts 15:2, the Church community of Antioch – decided to lay the question before a meeting of reputable men of note from the mother Church of Jerusalem. Acts and Galatians differ in their accounts of the settlement of the dispute. Paul (in Galatians 2:9–10) claims that James, Cephas (Peter) and John, who were jointly recognized as the pillars of the Jerusalem Church, simply offered a gentlemen's agreement that they would evangelize the Jews, and Paul and his companions the Gentiles. Their only specific requirement was that Paul should remember the poor of the Jewish churches, which he notes he intended to do anyway. Acts 15, however, gives a much more structural account in which the whole assembly make a decision set out in a formal letter with rather more restrictions imposed upon the Pauline party. Which is the more accurate account is not a question which can be settled here (if indeed it can be settled anywhere). It is much more important to recognize that the points in dispute were not laid before some already formed disciplinary or doctrinal structure claiming to act with the authority of Jesus or the 'apostles'. Faced with this extremely serious question involving the Christians' basic understanding of the fundamental nature of the Church community, that community had to feel its way to a conclusion through meeting and dialogue. From this procedure, of course, an authority structure began to evolve, but it is essential to realize that such structure was a matter of evolution from Church practice and not of prescription from divine command.

Paul himself certainly did not emerge from this experience with a conviction that Jesus had previously appointed an authority structure for the whole Church. The only authority structure he seems to have recognized consisted first, of himself, then the quasi-team which worked with him and finally, in a certain sense, all the Christian communities themselves, which are offered as models of Christian belief and conduct for each other. Certainly, Paul nowhere shows any recognition of such an authority, even Cephas', superior to himself and no one in that dispute argued that they had prior authority from Jesus to settle disputes. Naturally enough, the embryonic authority structure which emerged from the affair sought increasingly to back-date its position to explicit provisions emanating from Jesus: that is human nature, not scriptural exegesis.

None of this is to be read as implying that 'apostles' are of no particular significance in the Church. We must, however, be wary of taking too simplistic a view of the constituents of this group. Traditionally, we speak and write of the 12 'apostles' whose names are listed in the Gospels. In fact, the New Testament takes a much wider view of what constitutes an authentic apostle than we perhaps realize. Even Luke, who in his Gospel consistently refers to just 'the twelve' as apostles, uses the term in a wider sense in Acts. In Acts 14: 4 & 14, Paul and Barnabas are described as apostles. Paul himself certainly considered himself to be an apostle and is, in general, willing to confer the name on anyone with a credible claim to have been sent (the basic meaning of the term) to preach the kingdom of God. In Romans 16:7, for instance, he sends greetings to 'those outstanding apostles, Andronicus and Junius'. Interestingly, the ancient manuscripts differ about the name Junius: variants are Junias, Junia and Julia, the last of which would certainly be female. The essential qualification in the New Testament for the title 'apostle' is having witnessed to the risen Jesus. This is obviously a group far larger than simply the twelve. Paul, for instance, in 1 Corinthians 15, writes of Jesus appearing 'to more than five hundred brethren at one time'. This would naturally include women among the apostles as authentic witnesses to the resurrection. Indeed, John's Gospel makes a major point of showing a woman, Mary Magdalene, as the *first* witness to the risen Christ.

We now need to ask what part this vital group played in the life of the early Church. Undoubtedly some of them were leaders in the community. Paul seems to have formed a 'management team' with Timothy and Sosthenes (see 1 Thessalonians 1:1) or with either of these men on his own (see Philippians 1:1, 2 Corinthians 1:1 and

1 Corinthians 1:1). In Acts 18:26, we find a husband *and wife* team co-operating in giving further instruction to Paul himself. In Paul's own letters, he mentions around 80 personal names of people, clearly regarded as 'apostles', who perform various functions in the service of the community. They are teachers or leaders, both male and female, evangelists, prophets and deacons. *Never* are they called priests, as we have noted earlier, and *nowhere* are they regarded as a hierarchical governing body instituted by Jesus. That is a later historical development.

It is important to realize that nothing that has been written here is intended to prove or even to suggest that the hierarchical structure of the Church which has developed historically is in itself opposed by or to the New Testament. The point to grasp is that it is simply not mentioned in it. The Church which emerged from the post-resurrection faith of the first believers was not organized on a hierarchical basis nor did anyone suggest that this was what Jesus intended. It was developed by the People of God as a response to the perceived needs of the community. It is, of course, humanly understandable that, once such a hierarchy had been established, those who wielded power in the system should wish to legitimize their power on the basis of an appeal to Jesus' intentions. As we have seen, such an appeal is supported by neither the Church's foundation documents nor the practice of its first members. It therefore follows that there is nothing unscriptural or antecedently opposed to the mind of Christ in seeking new structures for the Church community in the entirely new situation in which it finds itself today.

Some Christians would, of course, like to free the Church from all structure, but this is, frankly, a foolish and indeed futile ambition. No community can survive without some formalization of its structure, from the local photographic club to the most complex political societies. The important principle is to ensure that whatever structure is erected, it has as its function the facilitation of the purposes of the particular society. Sadly, this principle, so far as the Church is concerned, gradually became obscured as the Church moved from being a loosely knit 'federation' of largely autonomous communities to something approaching the rigid, highly centralized structure that it has become today. As we have seen, the first Christian communities organized themselves on the familiar basis of their own Graeco-Roman and Jewish cultures. This might, incidentally, suggest that the current hostility of the Roman authorities to any suggestion that democracy has a legitimate place in the Church is sadly misplaced. Democracy is the most favoured social structure of *our* times and its desirability is surely enhanced by the New Testament emphasis upon the equality of all Christians. As Matthew 23:8 records of Jesus: 'You ["the crowds and his disciples"], however, must not allow yourselves to be called Rabbi, since you have only one Master, and you are all brothers.' Within these communities, no distinction was made between 'ministry' and 'service', as though 'ministers' were in some sense placed 'over' the community. All were for the building up of the community in Christ.

Leadership and authority there certainly were, but any such claim to such leadership or authority could be justified only by an authentically Christian character, a title which canon lawyers would find extremely difficult to define in legal terms: law always prefers more easily identifiable concepts. The convenience of lawyers, however, is not necessarily to be identified with the requirements of the Gospel. St Paul, for instance, claims a formal authority, not from documentary evidence of formal appointment but from his conviction that he was called directly by the Lord. It is important to insist, if we are adequately to meet the needs of today's Church, that such leadership was seen as one of many forms of service and not something set over and against other forms of service. There was a very real sense that all forms of service were under the direct tutelage of Jesus.

The passage of time saw a gradual shift from this rather more informal leadership, based very largely upon the charism of the Spirit, to an institutionalized local leadership. The position adopted by the elders ('episkopoi'), presbyters and deacons – who it is perhaps necessary to repeat are not to be identified with the bishops, priests and ordained deacons of today – in community disputes, increasingly became accepted orthodoxy, with the prophets and other more charismatic leaders losing their authority. Parallel with this development, the original house community became 'the household of God'. In this group, there was no longer a free association of equals with various authorities based on the presence and action of the Spirit, but a formal community subject to one authority: the 'episkopos' or presbyter. These in turn tended to form a kind of administrative council called the presbyterion, consisting of heads of households – which might of course include women. The episkopos is described as the leader, appointed perhaps in rotation. The post-Pauline 1 Timothy 5:17, for instance, holds that 'Elders who do their work well while they are in charge earn double reward, especially those who work hard at preaching and teaching'.

The Essence of Ministerial Priesthood

In this increasingly centralized bureaucracy, women quickly lost the place and dignity they had been accorded in Galatians 3:28. They were ordered to keep silent in the assembly and to seek wisdom from their husbands at home. This was in order not to offend the cultural sensibilities of the new, Gentile converts to Christianity. Already, the revolutionary ethos of the Gospel was yielding to the cultural demands of the age. The thrust of the books of Timothy and Titus is the importance of respectable religious practice, which will do nothing to offend the non-Christian neighbour and so increase the possibility of conversion. But, we may reasonably ask, what *kind* of conversion?

The process of ecclesiastical development from an informal, charismatic structure to our present rigid hierarchical organization can be linked to two famous personalities of the early Church. The first is Clement of Rome, notable for his Letter written around AD 92. Certain presbyters in Corinth had been deposed from office by a group of young men. Their character is uncertain: they may have been youths, or new converts or a group of deacons. Clement described the presbyters' deposition as illegitimate because it was contrary to the tradition that presbyters should be chosen by the whole community. It could be lawful only if the whole community judged that they had failed in their office and it is the community which must decide what is to be done. The letter then goes on to suggest that the *authority* of these presbyters, even though they are chosen by the community, is in fact derived from the apostles and it stresses throughout the need for obedience (for which, incidentally, the women of Corinth are particularly praised).

A Priestless People?

Certain points need to be noted about this letter. First of all, Clement – himself a presbyter – is anxious to defend his own status; hence the emphasis upon the permanence of his position. His description of how the apostles handed on their authority to others in an orderly, structured fashion, is derived from his own assertion and not at all from documentary evidence. As we have seen, such documentary evidence as is available suggests not only that there was no such organized system for the transference of authority, but also that Clement's notion of structural authority is a post-apostolic development and therefore could not have been derived from the apostles. Indeed, the general picture which emerges from the New Testament is that the apostles did not envisage the Church continuing much beyond their own lifetime; they would not therefore have been greatly concerned with the question of succession to their position or powers.

Secondly, the letter is wholly irrelevant to the discussion crucial to the theme of this book, that of the origin of the present day Church's understanding of powers said to be possessed by priests which mark them off as essentially different from the rest of the people of God.

The second personality is Ignatius of Antioch, who died in AD 107. He clearly distinguished the episkopos from presbyters and deacons, describing him as 'the permanent, truly episcopal president of the presbyteral college and therefore of higher rank'. In this position, the episkopos is established as a centre of Church unity. Interestingly, Ignatius does not describe this arrangement as a system inaugurated by the apostles, for the obvious reason that there is not the slightest trace in the New Testament of their having either done so or having even wished to do so. Ignatius asserted that it is an arrangement directly modelled on God's relationship with the world in Christ, with the Bishop (episkopos) corresponding to God, the deacons to Christ and the presbyters to the apostles. Moreover, in this scheme – according to Ignatius – the episcopate has taken over not the apostles' authority – for theirs is unique – but that of the early Christian prophets. In the hierarchical organization of the Church as outlined by Ignatius' powerful theological imagination, it is the charism of prophecy which has become institutionalized. We do not have here, therefore, either a New Testament situation or an organic development from the New Testament, but a new historical shift. As the fourth- or fifth-century Roman jurist and scriptural commentator, Ambrosiaster, remarks (approvingly, of course), the new Church order marked a break with the New Testament.

We should not imagine that Ignatius' model for Church order was the sole pattern for the time. At the end of the first century, the *Didache* (a document on Church order) still left prophets with an authority which was said to be above all criticism. They were leaders in the liturgy and authorized to preside at the Eucharist 'in a free way'. The final version of this document allowed the community to nominate episkopoi or deacons to preside at the Eucharist if no prophets were present. The New Testament, of course, contains no instructions as to who is to preside at the Eucharist and these ancient non-scriptural sources indicate that it was the task of the prophets and teachers, persons who were not identified in any very specific way.

Obviously, this is a very summary account of the early development of hierarchical power in the Church. But it surely must indicate to our ordinary fellow Catholics that

the received Western and perhaps particularly British picture of priesthood as the monopoly of celibate males deriv-
ing very distinct powers from the apostles by the will of
Christ via the authority of the Popes and the bishops lacks
historical and theological justification. Church authority,
obviously unintentionally, has in fact created a vocations
crisis by taking too narrow a view of priesthood. The implication of what is said here – and we do earnestly hope
that it will be taken up at wider, higher and more effective
levels – is that the Church already has within it the
resources to meet the vocations crisis. There is every reason
to believe that there are plenty of men and women able
and willing to minister to God's people and to the world
in sacrament and word. Nothing in either our foundation
documents or in the history of the first Christians bars us
from opening the exercise of Christ's priesthood, his gift
to the whole Church, both to men and to women – married
or single – and doing so without such restrictions as forbidding the single men and women among the candidates from
subsequent marriage. Nothing in those same documents or
history excludes the possibility of the community being
able to benefit from such priestly ministry for an agreed
temporary period or on a part-time basis. The Spirit of
God blows where she wills. Trust in that same Spirit should
surely calm fears that such a fresh approach to priesthood
will lower standards and weaken the force of the Gospel,
especially in the face of the fact that the present insistence
on a male, celibate priesthood is leading to the paralysis
and even erosion of Christian life in all quarters of the
globe.

I should like to end this book with a direct plea, first to

the authorities of our Church. For many years now, you have been appealing to parents to encourage their sons to think of becoming priests; you have made direct appeals to the boys and young men themselves; you constantly exhort us all to pray for vocations. These appeals and exhortations have manifestly proved ineffective. It would not be succumbing to a sinful spirit of the age, but a wise reading of the signs of the times, to take a fresh view of the crisis and at least strive to examine the possibility of fresh solutions. You declare your belief in the protection and guidance of the Holy Spirit: should not the sincerity of that declaration be put to the proof by a radically new approach?

Secondly, I would appeal to my fellow Catholics to awaken to their responsibilities, which are their privileges, as fully constituent members of the Church. Down the centuries, the task of the lay person has been seen, and – let us frankly admit – by the lay person happily seen, as simply carrying out the instructions issued by the hierarchy, or as raising money. This attitude is admirably summed up in the old description of the lay person's task as kneeling before the altar, sitting below the pulpit and putting their hand into their pocket or purse. The current shortage of priests is undoubtedly helping to erode this attitude, but its underlying ethos remains. Lay people must learn that they are full members of the Church and that the fulfilment of its mission is just as much their responsibility as that of the full-time, clerical officials whom we have come to expect to execute our duty on our behalf.

The work of the Church is to facilitate the coming of the Kingdom, and to the fulfilment of that work, all members of the Church are called. For some, the precise nature of that call is surely to share in a particular way in the priesthood of Christ committed to the Church by presiding at the regular eucharistic celebration in the midst of the community. But to make provision of the Eucharist, certainly ordained by Jesus Christ, the Son of God, wait upon the supply of personnel whose conditions of service are decided simply by the human authorities of the Church, is to invert Gospel values to a degree which can lead only to catastrophe for the Church's mission to the world – and the signs of that catastrophe are plain for us all to see.

Epilogue:

A Personal Retrospective

Lord, who shall we go to?
You have the message of eternal life.
(John 6:68)

Vincent and I completed the writing of this book in July 1995, and were beginning to look around for a publisher. We were well aware that this would be a difficult task, especially for a book which might only be of interest to a limited group of readers. Nevertheless, we both felt that what we had experienced over many years might help others in similar circumstances to think and pray about the priesthood.

So often nowadays we hear of priests leaving the ministry for various reasons and not being replaced, but until it happens to us personally we do not always appreciate the gravity of the situation.

In October that year our world was shattered when we were told that Vincent had cancer; we knew that he had only months to live. We decided not to hide our news and so we wrote to all our family and friends to tell them. We were to receive so much loving support from them all, which we both greatly needed.

We realized that it would be a great mistake to make comparisons with how things used to be or how we would like them to be again. We simply tried to take each day as it came and make the most of it. The curious thing was that we found this was a reality for everyone, not just the seriously ill. It was only when the future was actually seen to be uncertain that we realized we did only have the present moment in which to live.

Our hopes and prayers for more time together were not answered and after much suffering, borne with great courage, Vincent died peacefully in my arms in July 1996. During those last months together the time was so precious that the book was put to one side.

In May 1992 Vincent had been invited by Andrew Brown, then the Religious Affairs Correspondent for *The Independent*, to write an article on marriage and the priesthood. This appeared in the 'Weekend' supplement of 16 May as the main feature article. We were overwhelmed both at the time and in the months and years that followed by all the phone calls and letters received after its publication, even from places as far away as Australia and South Africa. We were made more aware of the suffering of so many other people. What moved us most was the great number of people who told us how much what Vincent had written had helped them to a greater understanding of the priesthood and the present situation in the Church. They also told us something we had known well for a long time: that many Catholics have little or no knowledge of how the law of celibacy came about. This Church law, which came into being in the twelfth century, was actually only binding on all ordained priests in the Western world, and *not* in the Eastern Rite where there are married priests – that is, until the Vatican has now set aside that rule for the Western world for the present in order to allow some married Anglican clergymen to be ordained into the Catholic Church. We are rightly asked to offer support and understanding to these men and their families, yet surely the same support and understanding should be given to our own priests who also wish to serve the community as married priests?

We found it was also news then, and incidentally still is to so many fellow Catholics, that over 100,000 priests world-wide had left the ordained priesthood since the time of the Second Vatican Council (1963–5) and the publication of the Papal Encyclical *Humanae Vitae* in 1968. It was because of this encyclical that after over four years of prayer and heart-searching, Vincent finally found that he could no longer in any way commend the Pope's teaching on the intrinsic immorality of artificial contraception to anyone. He therefore felt an obligation to make plain his own belief in any reference to the matter – that Catholics could, without subjective or objective sin, disagree with this teaching. That the Pope, most of the bishops and very many priests would have profoundly different opinions was obvious; in June 1972 his Archbishop told him that 'the only honest course would be to relinquish your pastoral ministry'.

This was a very painful and costly decision for Vincent to have to make, but he felt to do otherwise would be to do violence to his conscience, and this he was unable to do.

In *The Tablet* and *Catholic Herald* (7 March 1997) it was reported that the Vatican had just issued practical guidelines for confessors to help them deal with Catholics who admit the use of contraceptive methods. This twenty-five page document, *Vademecum for Confessors*

A Priestless People?

Concerning Some Aspects of the Morality of Conjugal Life, published by the Pontifical Council for the Family on 1 March 1997, urges priests to treat married couples who use contraception with 'mercy, discretion and respect'. The text states that the Church has always taught 'the intrinsic evil of contraception, that is of every marital act intentionally rendered unfruitful' and adds that 'this teaching is to be held as definitive and irreformable'. The manual then goes on to warn the confessor to 'avoid demonstrating lack of trust either in the grace of God or in the disposition of the penitent by exacting humanly impossible absolute guarantees of an irreproachable future conduct'. It is hard to understand what this document means exactly, but no doubt it will be widely debated.

What a tragedy it is for the Catholic Church that it has had to suffer the loss of so many of its finest priests whose voices were ignored over so many years because of this issue, and who only sought to give people help in forming their own consciences in these matters. For those whose life was not touched by the *Humanae Vitae* Encyclical there would have been little impact at the time. For others, their life was to be radically changed, and its consequences would never be forgotten. This was especially true for those priests who studied its contents and felt in all conscience that they could not commend it to their people.

At this time twelve priests were suspended throughout Britain, five from the Nottingham Diocese. One of these, a priest for twenty years, was asked to leave his presbytery within three days by the then Bishop, Edward Ellis. Another was allowed a slightly longer time because there was no one available to replace him. Three more were also suspended. None has been re-instated and Bishop Ellis, who did not like the publicity which surrounded these priests, thought it should be kept a private matter. The laity who loved their priests thought otherwise. The details of what happened in Nottingham are documented in *Four Honest Men – A Report by the Committee of the Catholic Renewal Group* (Partisan Press Ltd). These were men of deep faith in God, who after years of dedicated service to the Church found themselves deprived of their priesthood and sometimes abandoned by their fellow priests. Their courage and that of those who offered them help at the time was an example to us all.

It is still a popular belief that most priests leave the priesthood because they wish to marry, but already in many cases there is a profound dissatisfaction and disagreement with the magisteriums' general approach to marriage, sexual morality and indeed certain basic aspects of human living. Vincent found a great chasm between the wonderful words of the fourth eucharistic prayer describing Christ's mission – 'To the poor he proclaimed the good news of salvation, to the prisoner, freedom, and to those in sorrow, joy' – and the effects which much of official teaching had on human lives. As a result of the tension created by this conflict, between what he was aware he was supposed officially to teach and uphold as a Catholic priest and what he actually believed, he felt he could no longer continue to work in the priesthood.

In October 1972 his petition for laicization was sent to Rome. In it he made no request for permission to marry, as this was not his reason for leaving, but when the Rescript (Rome's written reply to a priest's application for laicization) came back the following year, permission to marry came with it. We were eventually therefore able to be married in my own Catholic parish church. We did not have to make an agonizing decision about our future life together, as have so many priests who wish to marry – since Pope John Paul II was elected, he has blocked almost all requests for this permission. I recently read a heart-rending letter from one such priest who has waited for four years for news of his dispensation which is still not forthcoming; meanwhile, he and his family are excluded from full participation in the liturgy. There are many hundreds of others who have waited far longer. After laicization is granted, it should surely not be left to the officials in Rome to decide if a man should or should not be allowed to marry. Would it be the will of God that a man who has found that he can serve God and others better as a married man should be treated in this way by fellow Christians?

Very many of us felt at the time of *Humanae Vitae* that we lost so many of our best and most compassionate priests. I am well aware that I would probably be accused of being prejudiced if I made that statement myself, but it has certainly been my own experience since Vincent's death. Those who I knew as caring priests and who subsequently left the priesthood and are now married are the ones who have been there without my asking for help. Could it be that marriage has brought them to a better understanding of the needs of their fellow Christians? There are also those still active in ministry whose help has sustained me over these last months. This is an opportunity to say to them all that the love and compassion they have shown have helped me to face the future, and to try to continue to be the person I have become since my life was touched by a priest who always treated women with respect, sympathy and great tenderness, who really understood how we feel, and who for twenty-three years brought to our marriage such deep and abiding love. They will know who they are and to them I will always be grateful.

I can write only from my own experience of a man who was asked to leave the priesthood and who, finding he could not be used in our own Church, set about sharing his talents with the wider Christian community. So our loss was to become their gain. He was welcomed with open arms by all the Christian churches in our area, to preach, to take services and to teach theology and scripture. We were invited to be present at the ordination of the first Anglican woman priest in our area, the Rev. Hilary Eve, and Vincent was honoured to be asked to preach at her first eucharistic celebration – a great ecumenical occasion. What she wrote of him in her church magazine after his death sums up what she and so many who attended his Requiem felt about him:

> It was an opportunity for all of us to reflect on the many gifts Vincent shared so generously with us, especially the gift of himself. It was a time to give thanks – for the inspiration, guidance and wisdom he brought to 'Churches Together in Coulsdon'; for his skill and ability in teaching – he had a gift for interesting others and challenging them without ever making them feel small; for his spiritual help and guidance given to so many whether through 'Quiet Days' which he led, Bible Studies and discussion groups, or individual help and counsel; for his preaching – sermons in which no one ever fell asleep and which sought both to guide and to make people think and reflect for themselves. And it was also time to give thanks for the personal qualities

that made Vincent the unique individual he was. He was a man of great integrity whose pursuit of truth and justice took him on some costly paths in his life, a man with a passion for justice who was angered both by greed and oppression and also by complacency. But he was also a person of compassion and kindness, one who spoke of a God of love and was himself loving and accepting. He was a person of deep faith – perhaps because he was never afraid to question and doubt – who lived out that faith seven days a week.

To so many people he was a friend – whose kindness, generosity and wonderful sense of humour as well as his sensitivity made it a pleasure to spend time with. For Vincent the journey has gone on into the peace and love of God's eternity and we have been left with memories to cherish and gifts to use.

I hope my ministry will be the better for all I learned from him.

The Reverend John Bown, the Methodist minister I invited to give the Homily at Vincent's Requiem, spoke of him in equally moving words:

The Gospel of Jesus Christ makes it clear that the Kingdom comes before anything else: all our other loyalties are secondary. Again and again Jesus said, 'Seek ye first the Kingdom of God.' We meet today to celebrate the life of one who believed this fervently, one who continually sought the Kingdom, one whose life reflected in many ways the very qualities required of those who would enter and live within the Kingdom of God.

There are those today from the parishes that he served

in who remember with gratitude his inspired preaching and teaching and his deep, loving pastoral care and concern. We thank God for Vincent, priest and pastor.

Those of us who knew Vincent well knew him to be a just and honest man. A man of integrity. A maxim by which he lived was, 'To your own self be true'. He was a man who felt that he could do no other than follow the leading of his God-given conscience in his constant quest for that truth which is at the heart of all things. And when that conscience and quest brought him into conflict with his Church, to the extent that he felt he could no longer fulfil his calling as a priest, it was with great sorrow that he resigned from the priesthood. Then no longer able to perform priestly duties, Vincent found other ways of serving his Church, the wider Christian community and the society in which he lived. Vincent continued to offer and use his gifts within the life of the Church. The churches and Christians of Coulsdon have a lot to thank God for today as we reflect on Vincent's ministry among us. To alter slightly and re-phrase a title given to one of Vincent's heroes of the past, St Thomas More, he was 'A man for all Churches'. He delighted in the company of other Christians, was frustrated – as most of us are – by those things which continue to separate us, but delighted in the measure of unity which has been achieved, particularly here in Coulsdon, and worked hard for its greater realization and fulfilment. Some words of Pope John XXIII, another of Vincent's heroes, could well be applied to himself: 'Whenever I see a wall between Christians I try to pull out a brick.' A few bricks have been removed by Vincent. Along with the apostle Paul in our epistle today, Vincent was a man of 'one Body and one Spirit'. We thank God for Vincent, friend and brother to all Christians.

These were but two of the many hundreds of tributes paid to Vincent. But I know that these tributes could be paid to many others I know personally, and I am sure it is true of many hundreds of priests who have been lost to the Church but who would have been and still would be able to carry out the Church's mission as married priests.

There was a plea from the Austrian bishop of a diocese deep in the Brazilian rainforest in *The Tablet* (1 March 1997) in which he said he 'considers the ordination of *viri probati*, or mature married men, an absolute necessity'. His diocese was four times the size of Austria, but had only twenty priests. There were six hundred scattered base communities, and he said that the people just did not understand why they could only celebrate the Eucharist every few months, or in some cases every two years. He also recalled that the Second Vatican Council had said that the Christian Community would only be built up if it were based and centred on the Eucharist. When a group of Latin American bishops visited Rome two years ago they wished the subject to be discussed but the request was not granted.

As a priest, Vincent touched so many lives – he was always there for people who needed him, showing them compassion and understanding. Many of the people who had sought his help as a priest continued to come to him for help and advice after he had left the parishes he had worked in, and many have become close friends. He was always willing to give of his time to those in need, and there were many. He found time to visit the sick, the lonely and the unhappy wherever he saw the need. He always seemed to be able to find time to do all the things required of a priest while never neglecting his home, his work and his prayers. As our love grew, his ability to understand and help others grew.

Vincent always felt that those studying for the priest-hood should be given the choice between celibacy and mar-riage. There will always be those who wish to embrace celibacy, that special gift given to some, a charism. There are also those who would dearly love to combine the priest-hood with marriage. In a programme on BBC 2 (5 March 1997), a priest suggested that between forty and ninety per cent of priests are at present in relationships. This of course can and will be disputed, but many of us know of priests in this situation. Even if we take the lower number as being more correct, it surely tells us of the problem and the damage done to the priests and the women concerned, damage that could easily be avoided. Something needs to be done quickly if the problem is to be resolved. Otherwise what happened with *Humanae Vitae* will happen over the rule of celibacy: instead of the sheep following the shepherd, we will find the shepherd again having to follow the sheep. This is a problem which will not go away, and which needs to be faced now by hierarchy and laity alike. It needs to be discussed openly by all concerned, with patience and understanding, and we should all pray for the guidance of the Holy Spirit. The law of celibacy was a Church law, found nowhere in the New Testament, and which came into being in the twelfth century for reasons which prevailed at that time. It could be changed tomorrow by those same Church authorities. It would surely make sense to bring the whole debate out in the open in order to prevent even more damage being done to the Church which these priests love and in which they wish to remain. With the acceptance of married Anglican priests by so many of us, surely the same acceptance should be offered to our own priests who wish to marry?

Vincent worked out his life despite all that was done to him by the official Church with great courage and always with forgiveness. He continually encouraged me to do the same and this I have always tried to do. It is a great grief to watch someone you love deeply being hurt by the Church you belong to and love. His mission in life was to help others to an understanding of the God who made us and to whom we must all return. There are many things, now allowed to lay people, which he would dearly have loved to have taken part in but which were denied to him as one who had left the priesthood; again, however, he accepted this. He was of course not alone in this. We see the official Church silencing theologians, priests and academics without a fair hearing, as in these last months we have witnessed the excommunication of Fr Tissa Bala-suriya, a greatly loved priest and respected theologian, whose book, *Mary and Human Liberation* was judged to contain grave errors. He has since lost his appeal against the judgement. If the Vatican is as deeply committed to the pursuit of justice and charity as it wishes us to believe, surely it must be seen that all these people, including the priests, have a right to be heard before they are condemned in the name of Christ?

Looking back over many years of personal struggles with the Church, I understand very clearly why people continued to need, trust and love Vincent in his last years, just as they did all those years ago, and why some continued to go to such lengths to find him in their hours of greatest need. From the earliest days in his priestly life he was a man who could take your hand and listen, really listen, to all that was needed to be said; this was and continued to be extended to all those who needed him. He had the rare ability in a priest not to be threatened by women, to really understand how we feel and how difficult it could be for some women to come and ask for help if they had been rejected in the past. Of course, we all know of priests who are able to do this too, but their number is decreasing; and, as often happens, several parishes have to be served by one priest who no longer has time available for the real needs of his people. An answerphone is no substitute for the real person, and these are in use more and more often.

In the first chapter of this book, which was written some four years ago, we speak of the decline of vocations in England, Wales and Scotland. That decline continues as statistics in both the National Catholic Directories show. The most recent figures for Scotland, published in *The Tablet* (15 March 1997), show a drop of more than half in the number of young men in the 'Vocations Scotland' scheme. A continuing decline in the number of priests and seminarians is shown in the annual statistics published in the 1997 Catholic Directory. The number of secular priests is down by 19 to 755 and of other priests by 10 to 180. This should be a cause of great concern to all the people of God.

We had felt there would be time in the future to deal with some of the complex reasons why so many priests have left and why so few men are coming forward to replace them. This is not now possible for us and my hope is that what has been written in this book will go some way towards giving people a better understanding of the complexities involved. This, I am sure, is never a sudden decision on the part of any priest but something that over months and maybe years causes much heartsearching, dialogue and prayer. It can never be easy to give up home and security for an unknown future; for priests who have this security and in many cases no other formal qualifications it must be a daunting prospect. They often have to face hostility from family and friends who do not understand why they have come to this decision. If they finally decide that in conscience this is what they must do, they should be welcomed into the community by priests and people and given the opportunity to use what talents they bring with them. None of us knows what is in the heart of others and we should never stand in judgement. What they decide to do surely is between them and God, to whom they must answer, and so we should accept them and treat them as we would wish to be treated ourselves – with understanding and love.

Some three years ago, Vincent was asked by the local Methodist church to write a profile of himself for their newsletter. He ended it with these words: 'I was born a Catholic, have lived as a Catholic and hope to die as a Catholic.' Despite all that he suffered he remained true to the Church he grew up in and never stopped loving. I pray that I and all those he has helped over the years will be given the grace and strength to follow his example.

After his death I found on his desk a list he had made of things to be done in the coming week, one of which was 'Find a publisher'. I know that it was one of his dearest wishes that this work would in some way help our fellow Catholics to understand that they, too, are fully members of the Church and have as much responsibility for its mission to facilitate the coming of the Kingdom as the hierarchy. He loved the Church and grieved to see what was happening to it and its members.

I received one letter after Vincent died from a serving priest whom I have never met, who feels that celibacy should not be made a condition for ordination to the priesthood. He said he had often wondered if he would have had the courage to do what so many priests felt they had to do at the time of *Humanae Vitae*. Among the many comforting things he wrote, the most moving for me were the words with which he ended his letter: 'Thank you for having helped make him fully human.' Vincent certainly thought that our marriage had brought a new dimension to his life which enabled him to serve God's people better.

I offer this book to all those like us who have suffered rejection and whose only wish is to follow their God-given consciences. We were always saddened to hear of priests who had been rejected by family and friends on leaving the ministry and getting married, and we prayed for the same understanding and love for them that we received from both our families from the time Vincent's decision to leave the priesthood had to be made to the following year when he asked me to marry him. They surrounded us with loving support without which life would indeed have been bleak. There are very many in similar situations who are sadly denied this by their relations, close friends and even fellow clergy at a time when it is most needed.

Our support came not only from family and close friends, but also from many of the parishioners from the parishes in which Vincent served and from the clergy and parishioners of all the Christian churches in Coulsdon. He was ever grateful for their continued love and confidence

in him and especially for their willing and loving acceptance of me. Those who continued to seek his help and
advice gave him the opportunity to continue to share his
gifts of deep faith, love and compassion. Many have
become part of our wider family and I thank them on his
behalf and my own. There were also some of his fellow
clergy who gave him their support, sometimes sadly at risk
to themselves from the authorities, but who understood
his decision, admired his courage and allowed him to use
his many talents. To them we were especially grateful.

We were much comforted by those priests who supported us so much in the last months of Vincent's life and
to one in particular for the understanding and acceptance
of our needs which I am sure were not always what he
might have expected, but who nevertheless always
respected our wishes and who gave so much of his time.
His coming and just being with me in the hours after Vincent died is something for which I will always be deeply
grateful. I now hope and pray for that same support to
help me to continue my lonely journey without Vincent.
He lives on in his wonderful work and I pray for the grace
to continue this work in the way he would have wished
me to.

I know Vincent would have wished me to record our
thanks to Christine Smith of the Canterbury Press for her
great kindness to me and her help in making it possible
for this book to be published. Her welcoming voice on
the telephone whenever I rang always conveyed to me the
impression that she was never too busy to listen and give
helpful and sound advice. This has been a great comfort
to me at this most painful time in my life.

Vincent changed my life in so many ways. He shared

his deep knowledge and love of scripture with me and encouraged me to read and study it with him; this was then shared with so many of our fellow Christians. He brought into our marriage all his many qualities and gifts and most of all his deep love: love of me, and love and compassion freely shared with all those whose lives he touched.

My greatest sorrow in life has been to see how Vincent was rejected so often by the official Church. My greatest blessing was to have been chosen by Vincent to be his wife and to have had the privilege of helping him in his work during the wonderful years we shared. As a priest and a husband he brought me to a closer understanding of the meaning of life. He is now in the peace and love of God's eternity, the God he loved and served so well. I dedicate this book to Vincent, with all my love.

Imelda McLaughlin
10 March 1997

Suggested Further Reading

Abbot, W.E. (ed.), *The Documents of Vatican II*, Geoffrey Chapman, 1966

Blenkinsopp, J. *Celibacy, Ministry, Church*, Burns & Oates, 1969

Brown, R.E. (ed.), *Peter in the New Testament*, Geoffrey Chapman, 1973

——, *The Churches the Apostles Left Behind*, Geoffrey Chapman, 1984

——, *The Community of the Beloved Disciple*, Geoffrey Chapman, 1979

Boff, Leonardo, *Church, Charism & Power*, SCM Press, 1985

——, *Ecclesiogenesis*, Collins, 1986

Cox, Harvey, *The Silencing of Leonardo Boff*, Collins, 1988

Curran, Charles, *Faithful Dissent*, Sheed & Ward, 1987

De Rosa, Peter, *Vicars of Christ*, Corgi, 1989

Dodd, C.H., *The Founder of Christianity*, Collins, 1971

Dominian, Jack, *Authority*, Darton, Longman & Todd, 1976

Fox, Matthew, *Original Blessing*, Bear & Co., 1983

Furlong, Monica, *A Dangerous Delight*, SPCK, 1991

Granfield Patrick, *The Papacy in Transition*, Gill & MacMillan, 1981

Suggested Further Reading

Guzie, Tad W., *Jesus and the Eucharist*, Paulist Press, 1974

Hasler, A.B., *How the Pope became Infallible*, Doubleday, 1981

Hebblethwaite, P., *John XXIII*, Geoffrey Chapman, 1984

——, *In the Vatican*, OUP, 1987

——, *Introducing John Paul II*, Fount, 1982

——, *Paul VI*, Fount, 1993

——, *The Next Pope*, Fount, 1995

Hill, Edmund, *Ministry and Authority in the Catholic Church*, Geoffrey Chapman, 1988

Kung, Hans, *Credo*, SCM Press, 1993

——, *Infallible?*, Fount, 1980

——, *On Being a Christian*, Collins, 1977

——, *The Church – Maintained in Truth*, SCM Press, 1979

——, *Truthfulness: The Future of the Church*, Sheed & Ward, 1968

——, *Why Priests?*, Fount, 1972

Jenkins, Clare, *A Passion for Priests*, Hodder Headline, 1995

Kaiser, R.B., *The Encyclical that Never Was*, Sheed & Ward, 1987

Lash, Nicholas, *His Presence in the World*, Sheed & Ward, 1968

McKenzie, John L., *Authority in the Church*, Geoffrey Chapman, 1966

Noonan, John T., *Contraception*, New American Library, 1965

Murphy, Annie, *Forbidden Fruit*, Warner, 1993

Pflieger, Michael, *Celibacy*, Sheed & Ward, 1967

Ranke-Heinemann, U., *Eunuchs for Heaven*, Deutsch, 1990

Rice, David, *Shattered Vows*, Blackstaff Press, 1991

Richards, H.J., *God's Diary*, Columba Press, 1991

Reuther, R.R., *Contemporary Roman Catholicism*, Sheed & Ward, 1987

——, *Sexism & God-Talk*, SCM Press, 1983

——, *To Change the World*, SCM Press, 1981

Schillebeeckx, E., *Clerical Celibacy Under Fire*, Sheed & Ward, 1968

——, *The Church with a Human Face*, SCM Press, 1985

Sheehan, M., *Apologetics and Catholic Doctrine*, M.H. Gill & Son, Revised 1950.

Vogels, Heinz-J., *Celibacy – Gift or Law*, Burns & Oates, 1992

Walsh, McEwan & Brewster, *Celibacy in Control*, Kathleen Fedouloff.

Wijngaards, J., *Did Christ Rule out Women Priests?*, Mayhew-McCrimmon, 1977

Winter, Michael, *Whatever Happened to Vatical II?*, Sheed & Ward, 1985

Wrage, K.H., *Man and Woman*, Collins, 1969